Nathartuka elay Al-Thawarti volume 2

By

Sayyar Isma'il Swift

إن الحمد لله نحمده و نستعينه و نستغفره و نعود بالله من شرور انفسنا و من سيئات أعمالنا من يهده الله فلا مضل له و من يضلل فلا هادي له و اشهد أن لا إله إلا الله وحده لا شريك له و ان محمدا عبده و رسوله

All thanks and praise is due to Allah, we seek his help and forgiveness. We seek refuge in Allah from the evil within ourselves and the consequences of our evil deed. Whoever Allah guides will never be led astray, and whoever Allah leads astray will never find guidance. I bear witness there is no God but Allah, alone without partners and alone is his worship; I also bear witness that Muhammad s.a.w. is his last prophet, slave & Messenger...

فَلَوْلَا كَانَ مِنَ الْقُرُونِ مِن قَبْلِكُمْ أُولُو بَقِيَّةٍ يَنْهَوْنَ عَنِ الْفَسَادِ فِي الْأَرْضِ إِلَّا قَلِيلًا مِّمَّنْ أَنجَيْنَا مِنْهُمْ ۗ وَاتَّبَعَ الَّذِينَ ظَلَمُوا مَا أُتْرِفُوا فِيهِ وَكَانُوا مُجْرِمِينَ

So why were there not among the generations before you those of enduring discrimination forbidding corruption on earth - except a few of those We saved from among them? But those who wronged pursued what luxury they were given therein, and they were criminals. [Al-Hud 11:116]

وَمَا كَانَ رَبُّكَ لِيُهْلِكَ الْقُرَىٰ بِظُلْمٍ وَأَهْلُهَا مُصْلِحُونَ

And your Lord would not have destroyed the cities unjustly while their people were reformers. [Al-Hud 11:117]

وَلَوْ شَاءَ رَبُّكَ لَجَعَلَ النَّاسَ أُمَّةً وَاحِدَةً ۖ وَلَا يَزَالُونَ مُخْتَلِفِينَ

And if your Lord had willed, He could have made mankind one community; but they will not cease to differ.[Al-Hud 11:118]

إِلَّا مَن رَّحِمَ رَبُّكَ ۚ وَلِذَٰلِكَ خَلَقَهُمْ ۗ وَتَمَّتْ كَلِمَةُ رَبِّكَ لَأَمْلَأَنَّ جَهَنَّمَ مِنَ الْجِنَّةِ وَالنَّاسِ أَجْمَعِينَ

Except whom your Lord has given mercy, and for that He created them. But the word of your Lord is to be fulfilled that, "I will surely fill Hell with jinn and men all together." [Al-Hud 11:119]

وَكُلًّا نَّقُصُّ عَلَيْكَ مِنْ أَنبَاءِ الرُّسُلِ مَا نُثَبِّتُ بِهِ فُؤَادَكَ ۚ وَجَاءَكَ فِي هَٰذِهِ الْحَقُّ وَمَوْعِظَةٌ وَذِكْرَىٰ لِلْمُؤْمِنِينَ

And each [story] We relate to you from the news of the messengers is that by which We make firm your heart. And there has come to you, in this, the truth and an instruction and a reminder for the believers. [Al-Hud 11:120]

وَقُل لِّلَّذِينَ لَا يُؤْمِنُونَ اعْمَلُوا عَلَىٰ مَكَانَتِكُمْ إِنَّا عَامِلُونَ

And say to those who do not believe, "Work according to your position; indeed, we are working.[Al-Hud 11:121]

وَانتَظِرُوا إِنَّا مُنتَظِرُونَ

And wait, indeed, we are waiting."[Al-Hud 11:122]

وَلِلَّهِ غَيْبُ السَّمَاوَاتِ وَالْأَرْضِ وَإِلَيْهِ يُرْجَعُ الْأَمْرُ كُلُّهُ فَاعْبُدْهُ وَتَوَكَّلْ عَلَيْهِ ۚ وَمَا رَبُّكَ بِغَافِلٍ عَمَّا تَعْمَلُونَ

And to Allah belong the unseen [aspects] of the heavens and the earth and to Him will be returned the matter, all of it, so worship Him and rely upon Him. And your Lord is not unaware of that which you do. [Al-Hud 11:123]

The driving force within society is Fear not Love...

Foreword

The following pages are meant to brief introduce readers into some of the fields of science and study on the well-being of our mental states, as well as point out some of the contrast that result to humanities illnesses. Utilizing verses from the Quran and saying from the beloved prophet Muhamad s.a.w. we compare secular views with that of Islamic viewpoints. On a variety of comparisons I briefly delve into some of the research on the topic enough to intrigue the reader into further exploration...

Nathartukum elay Al-Thawarti vol. 2

Perception is the Commodity

Psychological look into the conformity of society...

By

Sayyar Isma'il Swift

[Student of knowledge/Psychology Major]

Compiled in Morocco 2016 ©

Cover Art work: Sayyar Isma'il Swift

ISLAMIC REFERENCES TAKEN FROM QURAN AND SUNNAH OF THE
PROPHET MUHAMMAD S.A.W IN AUTHENTIC, SAHIH CLASSED AHADITH,
OF THE MAJOR COMPILERS OF HADITH.

Table of Contents

Foreword

Passively sitting back allowing, watching and for some it's a source by which they're entertained or profit from. Engulfed in flames that are spreading around the world in human turmoil, the cry out towards injustices has never been so great yet seemingly unheard... All society is socially constructed, so when we see those of us taking to the sidelines or those of us who have dropped out of the fight from hopelessness or selfishness then we have to remember that

each condition is a pixel that helps to bring that larger picture into full view. Large still is the global effort which has long been burning in gaining control of the world geo-politically, but now the flames have spread to regions that were responsible for its setting to begin with. Among us as it appears, but not with us as they manipulate the entire way of life usurping not just money out of the economy to further tighten their grip upon humanity; but in addition they usurp & exploit our time, energies, as well as body-parts/DNA etc. Limitations have no boundaries to how far they are willing to push their campaign towards meeting it goals, however be assured that the more evil things become it is an indication to just how close they have become to reaching their goals by setting the world ablaze...

Competition vs Co-operation

Figure 1 cooperation vs competition

Some might argue the natural state of humanity, but historically our natures all lean toward cooperative model. All throughout history people have collectively worked together in gathering food, building their dwellings, and aiding each for the benefit of themselves as well as the whole. Understanding that survival was indeed hinge on the well-being of others, it was then second nature to be in cooperative states. Ironically enough for argument sakes even if we consider the competitive model, in order to be highly competitive we still require the cooperation of the smaller group(s) to bring about that success. Why? Well its simple, we can of our own selves do nothing. For example: Any of our modern corporations still have within them small groups who collectively cooperate in order to compete with other collected groups in formation of corporations in bringing their goods to market. Thus I find it so that cooperation is the fundamental basis that is absolutely necessary in order to have civilized life & for the sustenance of life. Competitions therefore arise out of cooperation, but by itself would find no way of self-existence...We find a good example within the Quran with the story about the ants who saw Prophet Sulaiman a.s. marching over the land with his army. She (the ant) warned her fellow ants to go down into their dwellings before Sulaiman a.s. and his army reached them... trampling them without acknowledgement. The verse is clear, but within it again we still find many other wisdoms about the ant which leads to confirm their known successes that we witness. We find in the verse her desire to warn the others from impeding danger. Understanding the importance of survival for the others directly impacts her own individual well-being. Also what we can gather from this is the responsibility she honored in warning her fellow ants towards harmful conditions approaching. Honoring that responsibility she encourages others to do the same, while at the same time the empathy holds tight the bond of the community as doing the opposite would surely create enmity from those who suffered lost potentially because she failed to warn those in her company. So, the fabric of cooperation is better enjoined when there is mutual love and respect for one's self & others...

وَحُشِرَ لِسُلَيْمَانَ جُنُودُهُ مِنَ الْجِنِّ وَالْإِنسِ وَالطَّيْرِ فَهُمْ يُوزَعُونَ

And gathered for Solomon were his soldiers of the jinn and men and birds, and they were [marching] in rows. [An' Naml 27:17]

حَتَّىٰ إِذَا أَتَوْا عَلَىٰ وَادِ النَّمْلِ قَالَتْ نَمْلَةٌ يَا أَيُّهَا النَّمْلُ ادْخُلُوا مَسَاكِنَكُمْ لَا يَحْطِمَنَّكُمْ سُلَيْمَانُ وَجُنُودُهُ وَهُمْ لَا يَشْعُرُونَ

Until, when they came upon the valley of the ants, an ant said, "O ants, enter your dwellings that you not be crushed by Solomon and his soldiers while they perceive not."[An 'Naml 27:18]

فَتَبَسَّمَ ضَاحِكًا مِّن قَوْلِهَا وَقَالَ رَبِّ أَوْزِعْنِي أَنْ أَشْكُرَ نِعْمَتَكَ الَّتِي أَنْعَمْتَ عَلَيَّ وَعَلَىٰ وَالِدَيَّ وَأَنْ أَعْمَلَ صَالِحًا تَرْضَاهُ وَأَدْخِلْنِي بِرَحْمَتِكَ فِي عِبَادِكَ الصَّالِحِينَ

So [Solomon] smiled, amused at her speech, and said, "My Lord, enable me to be grateful for Your favor which You have bestowed upon me and upon my parents and to do righteousness of which You approve. And admit me by Your mercy into [the ranks of] Your righteous servants." [An 'Naml 27:19]

Watching the ants, and understanding the formula of cooperation it should be fairly easy to see the relationship of human progression from tribal life, to smaller individual communities to today's metropolises...Each is built & relies on the foundation of cooperation for its sustenance to function cohesively and collectively. Although modern with technological advancements, it still takes the same logistics to complete the overall functions of our mega-cities today. What

Figure 2 collective cooperation makes the city work

has gotten complicated is the management of things as everything has grown much bigger and produced much faster often exceeding demand or disposable income that would otherwise predict or determine demand. Seeking more control over the market share corporations [(Cartel(s) or monopolies are illegal)] have created the premise for greed & competition. In addition governments who were established for societal regulations have turned criminal in opposition to the freedoms to the individuals' sovereignty. Imposing principals to rearrange the societal landscape from voluntary cooperation in which we all have the freedoms of participation to involuntary, necessity derived from servitude based agenda that has evolved from behind the veil. As a result cooperation is now forced on (debt slaves) who have traded independency of land ownership to dependency of city living and grouped into companies of various sizes who compete for market share in turn providing a wage that keeps most people locked into their meniscal roles. This deception is embedded within the capitalistic model widening the gap between rich & poor. The nature of the system itself is rooted in greed because all acting participants aren't compensated in the same way that they would be if they had brought that same skill, knowledge, talents to market themselves; however it's influential when it puts within reach materials gains and surroundings of modern development for a population to be misled in attaining its heights. Don't be so quickly sold on the idea without understanding these small but very important principals. It is a top-down service system that feeds the smaller percentage at the top…Thinking outside the box like most employers, educators etc. like to talk about, is merely a concept of competitive recruitment into the trap of a larger box that works towards the advantage of the power elite.

We may differ in language, shapes, ethnicity etc. but we (humanity) were never meant to differ in belief nor on accordance to our true purpose in this creation nor in our duties towards one another & society/creation at large. Humanity was meant to be in one accordance as we see in the ants…the creator is ONE, humanity differs but we are all children of Adam, and the way of life is submission to the system in which was created for us to live by under divine governance. If people were to examine closely all the revelation each given to different prophets of different tongues, each called to the same way of life in correcting their respective nations from the misguidance they were upon…

وَمِنَ النَّاسِ مَن يَقُولُ آمَنَّا بِاللَّهِ وَبِالْيَوْمِ الْآخِرِ وَمَا هُم بِمُؤْمِنِينَ

And of the people are some who say, "We believe in Allah and the Last Day," but they are not believers. [2:8]

يُخَادِعُونَ اللَّهَ وَالَّذِينَ آمَنُوا وَمَا يَخْدَعُونَ إِلَّا أَنفُسَهُمْ وَمَا يَشْعُرُونَ

They [think to] deceive Allah and those who believe, but they deceive not except themselves and perceive [it] not. [2:9]

فِي قُلُوبِهِم مَّرَضٌ فَزَادَهُمُ اللَّهُ مَرَضًا ۖ وَلَهُمْ عَذَابٌ أَلِيمٌ بِمَا كَانُوا يَكْذِبُونَ

In their hearts is disease, so Allah has increased their disease; and for them is a painful punishment because they [habitually] used to lie.[2:10]

وَإِذَا قِيلَ لَهُمْ لَا تُفْسِدُوا فِي الْأَرْضِ قَالُوا إِنَّمَا نَحْنُ مُصْلِحُونَ

And when it is said to them, "Do not cause corruption on the earth," they say, "We are but reformers."[2:11]

أَلَا إِنَّهُمْ هُمُ الْمُفْسِدُونَ وَلَٰكِن لَّا يَشْعُرُونَ

Unquestionably, it is they who are the corrupters, but they perceive [it] not.[2:12]

وَإِذَا قِيلَ لَهُمْ آمِنُوا كَمَا آمَنَ النَّاسُ قَالُوا أَنُؤْمِنُ كَمَا آمَنَ السُّفَهَاءُ ۗ أَلَا إِنَّهُمْ هُمُ السُّفَهَاءُ وَلَٰكِن لَّا يَعْلَمُونَ

And when it is said to them, "Believe as the people have believed," they say, "Should we believe as the foolish have believed?" Unquestionably, it is they who are the foolish, but they know [it] not. [2:13]

وَإِذَا لَقُوا الَّذِينَ آمَنُوا قَالُوا آمَنَّا وَإِذَا خَلَوْا إِلَىٰ شَيَاطِينِهِمْ قَالُوا إِنَّا مَعَكُمْ إِنَّمَا نَحْنُ مُسْتَهْزِئُونَ

And when they meet those who believe, they say, "We believe"; but when they are alone with their evil ones, they say, "Indeed, we are with you; we were only mockers {of those who believe}."[2:14]

اللَّهُ يَسْتَهْزِئُ بِهِمْ وَيَمُدُّهُمْ فِي طُغْيَانِهِمْ يَعْمَهُونَ

[But] Allah mocks them and prolongs them in their transgression [while] they wander blindly.[2:15}

أُولَـٰئِكَ الَّذِينَ اشْتَرَوُا الضَّلَالَةَ بِالْهُدَىٰ فَمَا رَبِحَت تِّجَارَتُهُمْ وَمَا كَانُوا مُهْتَدِينَ

Those are the ones who have purchased error [in exchange] for guidance, so their transaction has brought no profit, nor were they guided.[2:16]

مَثَلُهُمْ كَمَثَلِ الَّذِي اسْتَوْقَدَ نَارًا فَلَمَّا أَضَاءَتْ مَا حَوْلَهُ ذَهَبَ اللَّهُ بِنُورِهِمْ وَتَرَكَهُمْ فِي ظُلُمَاتٍ لَّا يُبْصِرُونَ

Their example is that of one who kindled a fire, but when it illuminated what was around him, Allah took away their light and left them in darkness [so] they could not see.[2:17]

صُمٌّ بُكْمٌ عُمْيٌ فَهُمْ لَا يَرْجِعُونَ

Deaf, dumb and blind - so they will not return [to the right path].[2:18]

أَوْ كَصَيِّبٍ مِّنَ السَّمَاءِ فِيهِ ظُلُمَاتٌ وَرَعْدٌ وَبَرْقٌ يَجْعَلُونَ أَصَابِعَهُمْ فِي آذَانِهِم مِّنَ الصَّوَاعِقِ حَذَرَ الْمَوْتِ ۚ وَاللَّهُ مُحِيطٌ بِالْكَافِرِينَ

Or [it is] like a rainstorm from the sky within which is darkness, thunder and lightning. They put their fingers in their ears against the thunderclaps in dread of death. But Allah is encompassing of the disbelievers. [2:19]

يَكَادُ الْبَرْقُ يَخْطَفُ أَبْصَارَهُمْ ۖ كُلَّمَا أَضَاءَ لَهُم مَّشَوْا فِيهِ وَإِذَا أَظْلَمَ عَلَيْهِمْ قَامُوا ۚ وَلَوْ شَاءَ اللَّهُ لَذَهَبَ بِسَمْعِهِمْ وَأَبْصَارِهِمْ ۚ إِنَّ اللَّهَ عَلَىٰ كُلِّ شَيْءٍ قَدِيرٌ

The lightning almost snatches away their sight. Every time it lights [the way] for them, they walk therein; but when darkness comes over them, they stand [still]. And if Allah had willed, He could have taken away their hearing and their sight. Indeed, Allah is over all things competent. [2:20]

وَمِنَ النَّاسِ مَن يُعْجِبُكَ قَوْلُهُ فِي الْحَيَاةِ الدُّنْيَا وَيُشْهِدُ اللَّهَ عَلَىٰ مَا فِي قَلْبِهِ وَهُوَ أَلَدُّ الْخِصَامِ

And of the people is he whose speech pleases you in worldly life, and he calls Allah to witness as to what is in his heart, yet he is the fiercest of opponents.[2:204]

وَإِذَا تَوَلَّىٰ سَعَىٰ فِي الْأَرْضِ لِيُفْسِدَ فِيهَا وَيُهْلِكَ الْحَرْثَ وَالنَّسْلَ ۗ وَاللَّهُ لَا يُحِبُّ الْفَسَادَ

And when he goes away, he strives throughout the land to cause corruption therein and destroy crops and animals. And Allah does not like corruption. [2:205]

وَإِذَا قِيلَ لَهُ اتَّقِ اللَّهَ أَخَذَتْهُ الْعِزَّةُ بِالْإِثْمِ ۚ فَحَسْبُهُ جَهَنَّمُ ۚ وَلَبِئْسَ الْمِهَادُ

And when it is said to him, "Fear Allah," pride in the sin takes hold of him. Sufficient for him is Hellfire, and how wretched is the resting place. [2:206]

زُيِّنَ لِلَّذِينَ كَفَرُوا الْحَيَاةُ الدُّنْيَا وَيَسْخَرُونَ مِنَ الَّذِينَ آمَنُوا ۘ وَالَّذِينَ اتَّقَوْا فَوْقَهُمْ يَوْمَ الْقِيَامَةِ ۗ وَاللَّهُ يَرْزُقُ مَن يَشَاءُ بِغَيْرِ حِسَابٍ

Beautified for those who disbelieve is the life of this world, and they ridicule those who believe. But those who fear Allah are above them on the Day of Resurrection. And Allah gives provision to whom He wills without account. [2:212]

كَانَ النَّاسُ أُمَّةً وَاحِدَةً فَبَعَثَ اللَّهُ النَّبِيِّينَ مُبَشِّرِينَ وَمُنذِرِينَ وَأَنزَلَ مَعَهُمُ الْكِتَابَ بِالْحَقِّ لِيَحْكُمَ بَيْنَ النَّاسِ فِيمَا اخْتَلَفُوا فِيهِ ۚ وَمَا اخْتَلَفَ فِيهِ إِلَّا الَّذِينَ أُوتُوهُ مِن بَعْدِ مَا جَاءَتْهُمُ الْبَيِّنَاتُ بَغْيًا بَيْنَهُمْ ۖ فَهَدَى اللَّهُ الَّذِينَ آمَنُوا لِمَا اخْتَلَفُوا فِيهِ مِنَ الْحَقِّ بِإِذْنِهِ ۗ وَاللَّهُ يَهْدِي مَن يَشَاءُ إِلَىٰ صِرَاطٍ مُّسْتَقِيمٍ

Mankind was [of] one religion [before their deviation]; then Allah sent the prophets as bringers of good tidings and warner's and sent down with them the Scripture in truth to judge between the people concerning that in which they differed. And none differed over the Scripture except those who were given it - after the clear proofs came to them - out of jealous animosity among themselves {*seeking superiority through nation & lineage tied to prophets and their given scripture, but all guidance was the same it only differed in law as mankind progressed*}. And Allah guided those who believed {*Faith is a gift upon the sincere NOT an acquisition of statement*} to the truth concerning that over which they had differed, by His permission. And Allah guides whom He wills to a straight path. [2:213]

Looking towards the Creation & ourselves we also see the cooperation model. The Sun & Moon both run in their orbits; in addition the night/day, the sky, the human body with the spirit all come together in cooperation...

أَوَلَمْ يَرَ الَّذِينَ كَفَرُوا أَنَّ السَّمَاوَاتِ وَالْأَرْضَ كَانَتَا رَتْقًا فَفَتَقْنَاهُمَا ۖ وَجَعَلْنَا مِنَ الْمَاءِ كُلَّ شَيْءٍ حَيٍّ ۖ أَفَلَا يُؤْمِنُونَ

Have those who disbelieved not considered that the **heavens and the earth were a joined entity**, and We separated them and made from water every living thing? Then will they not believe? [Al-Anbiyah 21:30]

وَجَعَلْنَا فِي الْأَرْضِ رَوَاسِيَ أَن تَمِيدَ بِهِمْ وَجَعَلْنَا فِيهَا فِجَاجًا سُبُلًا لَّعَلَّهُمْ يَهْتَدُونَ

And We placed within the earth **firmly set mountains, lest it should shift with them**, and We made therein [mountain] passes [as] roads that they might be guided. [Al-Anbiyah 21:31]

وَجَعَلْنَا السَّمَاء سَقْفًا مَّحْفُوظًا ۖ وَهُمْ عَنْ آيَاتِهَا مُعْرِضُونَ

And We made the **sky a protected ceiling**, but they, from its signs, are turning away. [Al-Anbiyah 21:31]

وَهُوَ الَّذِي خَلَقَ اللَّيْلَ وَالنَّهَارَ وَالشَّمْسَ وَالْقَمَرَ ۖ كُلٌّ فِي فَلَكٍ يَسْبَحُونَ

And it is He who created **the night and the day and the sun and the moon; all [heavenly bodies] in an orbit are swimming**. [Al-Anbiyah 21:33]

What we find in cooperation is harmony, the natural agreeance upon divine stature in which all things have been created. Look at it this way...In competition one wins and one loses, but humanity is not meant to lose, any of us. Just from that simple definition we can understand that competition is something that is in opposition to harmony, and it's not sustainable over long periods of time. Some research conducted on the theory was done by David Johnson, a University of Minnesota Professor with some colleagues who sought to compile all the data they could find on the subject of cooperation vs competition from 1924 to 1980. They uncovered that 65% of the studies found that children learn better when they work cooperatively as opposed to competitively; and the more difficult the task the worse children in a competitive environment fared. In environments that are less competitive and more so cooperative you will find the removal of hostilities, envies, and self-defeating doubts which promote a far more relaxed environment where people are not pressured in achievement. Optimal arousal can thereby be attained according to ones abilities and sustained bringing more productivity & creativity to the table. Too much emphasis has been put on the need of being #1, as well as promoting the use of competition to increase creativity but it couldn't be further from the truth. Since most people lose in competition, it is a precursor to undermining overall success, raising doubt, and provoking stressful conditions more so than the beneficial factor.

Scientific research today has discovered just how interconnected we are by watching the brain as it fires in observance to stimulus in experimentation. To their surprise they found that while we observe empathic situations we aren't only in observation, we are in fact sharing the experience with those we see. The research showed that the same areas of the brain fire in our own brains for those very same emotions we are observing as if we were undertaking the same experience. This deepens our connection to others by allowing us to experience what we see in others. For me it further cements the definition of harmony and our inter-relatedness, interdependence and inter-connectedness…

Prior to 19th century research the consideration of purpose and plan of our existence was disregarded mostly from the inability to measure empirical data such as this brain behavior observation. The mind was something banned from biology and even the behavioral & social sciences. Gregory Bateson was one of the first scholars to appreciate the patterns of organization and relational symmetry evident in all living systems which were indicative to mind. He formulated the cybernetic epistemology as an overarching discipline of the natural sciences, including behavioral, social & meta-sciences which boundaries stretch to the outer most limits of containing its furthest understandings. (Bale, 1992) What he suggested was these relationships of our mental interconnected, interrelated & interdependencies embody a collective mind. This collective mind regulates the behavior within and between its members through observation & interaction with the outside… This collected regulation that is designed to govern harmony & cooperation brings me first to the idea of the golden mean ratio. The special number found within all creation…Found by dividing a line into two parts so that the longer part is divided by the smaller part which is also equal to the whole length divided by the longer part.

$$\rho = \frac{1 + \sqrt{5}}{2} = 1.6180339887\ldots$$

Figure 3 golden mean equation

Figure 4 pictorial representation

Often popularly accredited to Fibonacci (1170–1250) who mentioned the numerical series now named after him in his *Liber Abaci*; the ratio of sequential elements of the Fibonacci sequence approaches the golden ratio asymptotically, but there is a host of others who also mentioned to some extent or by having stumbled across the ratio unknowingly dating back to Phidias (490-430 BC) as well as Plato (427-347 BC). However, the concept in its full knowledge is something that the Creator has put into creation from the very beginning. Phi to 15 places is 1.6180339887499. There are 180 degrees between the North Pole and the South Pole, so 180 divided by Phi is 111.2461179749810. As latitudes are expressed in degrees and distance from the Equator, we subtract 90 degrees and convert this to a latitude of 21 degrees, 14 minutes and 46.02 seconds, North or South.

The latitude of Mecca, according to Google Earth, is 21 degrees, 25 minutes and 38.56 seconds. This puts it only 10 minutes and 52.54 seconds north of the exact northern golden ratio latitude of the Earth. This is a variance of less about 1/10 of a percent, about 12 miles or 20 kilometers north of the exact golden ratio latitude point. (Meisner, 2012) Considering what takes place each year in Mecca (the world's largest human gathering of the Hajj) we can clearly see the defining points of or interconnected, interrelated & interdependence outlined in the significance and placement of the first house of worship established for humanity. From the beginning of the verse to end of the word Mecca there is 29 letters, and from Word Mecca to end of the verse there is 18 letters. We see clearly golden ration in the position of Mecca, and Quranic verse about Mecca.

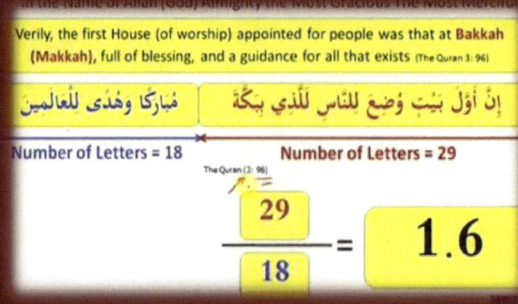

Figure 5 golden mean in verse that talks about Mecca and the Ka'bah

What is even more fascinating is science is now able to conduct experiments which confirm scripture of the Quran as well as these phenomena that are campaigned against in further disuniting humanity. In 2003, Volkmar Weiss and Harald Weiss analyzed psychometric data and theoretical considerations concluded that the golden ratio underlies the clock cycle of brain waves. In 2008 this was empirically confirmed by a group of neurobiologists (Weiss, 2003). Last to mention, but surely not last on the infinite number of evidences that present the same confirming data is the mention of the genome. The symmetry of our shapes and spacing of extremities all point to the same ratio, which we have now dubbed the finger print of Allah, the creator of all things...

Islam's system

Islam seeks to address the systematic details of our existence in maintaining this collective harmony of cooperation amongst human-beings as well as the animal kingdoms and creation. This is the premise behind shari'ah law (Arabic for divine law, the same you would find in the Torah & Injeel). Islam is the only system by which entire life can be sustained and prosper justly, and the evidence lies within history as well as the failings of human systems that have always tried intervening. The ages in which the world underwent the most progressive changes were in fact the ages attributed to Prophets are the guidance they had cemented within society as it governing system...Prophet/King David a.s., Prophet/King Sulaiman a.s. and the age of Islam after the Prophet s.a.w won his battles against idolatry that had settled in Arabia lasting until the early 1920's with the prophetic model of the caliphate. Of course the caliphate model was long before the 20's corrupted, by those seeking to break once again free of divine rule over humanity, unfortunately its undoing has always been done from within which helps to smear its image especially today in the age of media... Stepping away from the prophets (peace on all of them) and their highly regarded character; we have only ourselves to blame for the corruption that would again creep back in with its variety of material influence, wealth, and relaxation from the standards {fiqh} that helped to bring about such great transformations.

Although it is divinely prescribed and perfected it takes humanity to implement it...And like other systems it to consist of many different parts (you and I) in contributing to its functionality. System dynamics is attributed to Professor Jay Forrester of M.I.T. founded in 1956. From his conceptualized analysis, he thought of the system in terms of its individual parts and their interaction with other parts in better understanding the system. Analyzing each component part helped to better understand the total function from an individual part perspective or variety of component groups that made up the whole; both analyses are very important as we again come to the idea & conclusion of the interrelated, interconnected & interdependences of everything in cooperative functioning. This relationship of interaction goes back to the concept Gregory Bateson had on the relationship(s) of parts takes on a mind of its own that I've mentioned. In theory, when these relationships are broken apart each member would carry within in itself the capacity, knowledge/information to re-construct the larger system...As animate organisms I take it one step further to include action/desire to construct the larger system; As Muslims this ideal hits home.

The Prophet Muhammad (peace be upon him) said: "The seeking of knowledge is obligatory for every Muslim." – [Al-Tirmidhi, Hadith 74] The Prophet Muhammad (peace be upon him) said: "One who treads a path in search of knowledge has his path to Paradise made easy by God..." –[Riyadh us-Saleheen, 245] The Prophet Muhammad (peace be upon him) said: "A servant of God will remain standing on the Day of Judgment until he is questioned about his (time on earth) and how he used it; about his knowledge and how he utilized it; about his wealth and from where he acquired it and in what (activities) he spent it; and about his body and how he used it." – [Al-Tirmidhi, Hadith 148]

The superiority of the learned over the devout is like that of the moon, on the night when it is full, over the rest of the stars. The learned are the heirs of the Prophets, and the Prophets leave (no monetary inheritance), they leave only knowledge, and he who takes it takes an abundant portion. – [Sunan of Abu-Dawood, Hadith 1631]

If each of us (Muslims) strove to reach high levels of obtaining the right knowledge then we would each hold the capacity to re-construct sub-systems (individual families, then communities) and then linking those sub-systems to the overall system. This is the major difference between us today in regards to the earlier generations; unlike ourselves when things began to deviate & operate outside of normal functionality they were able to reconstruct the whole by their own individual capacities {Early scholars fought deviation with knowledge}... Because it's an open system, Islam has always been the target of inside corruption aimed at altering its perception, which is a credit to its truth & strength. In addition, as new Muslims accept the truth they often bring with them working ways & ideals of their pre-existing systems which cause misfires with the finely tuned engine parameters of Islam. Hence the need of further knowledge and watchfulness over new Muslims to ensure they gain the appropriate knowledge that they will be able also to reconstruct the perfection already outlined for us.

Severely demonized and headless in leadership, the body stands but finds it difficult obviously to move, think or respond accordingly without a head...Nonetheless the feedback loops on the micro scale have all been suggesting that the behavior and interactions of these member relationships change course. When bombarded over & over again with the same none concluding issues these patterns have to be negotiated until a consensus can be found in implementing change from previous norms to better interrelations amongst parts. Current patterns of dysfunction seem only to be unsatisfactory to a few, which is a common negative quality. Resistant to change, and persuaded outside cooperation often for reasons that are competitive, rocking the boat to provoke change is resisted even though we all can see the dysfunction of the whole.

Systems have a tendency then to return back to their former status {hemostasis} when the information fed back to it isn't critically examined against the established behavior of the organism...especially if that status has endured allowing individuals to become complacent unto its proper discipline and settled in laziness. Therefore, while in one state members should be working to help alter its state to a better one accepting change and understanding that it's inevitable. The current pathology of etiology is of course deviation from knowledge, and more so exercising that knowledge in reconstructing the condition(s) of normalcy within the micro & then macro system according to Quran/Sunnah.

The very title is intriguing enough as if it is something not yet, but rather lingering on the cusp of being triggered.

The controversy surrounded the publishing of the 2013, 5th edition of the Diagnostic & Statistics Manual of Mental Disorders (DSM-5) on whether personality disorders should be defined as categorical entities or combinations of extreme personality dimension. This trait-based approach is also described in the International Classification of Diseases 11th revision (ICD-11). Largely neglected in the past in adolescents and young adults primarily for incomplete formation of identity, recent epidemiological studies from a multi-wave increase suggesting worst problems for those whose symptoms have endured through adolescence; as a result the psychopathology presiding over it for the last year has been regarded to NOT be a transient phenomenon (Carla Sharp, 2015). Again, the name tends to imply a great deal of its suggestive findings geared at better understanding our youth. One such diagnosis was made over a 6 to 36 month time span where one hundred outpatients were monitored for this phenomological development. Family histories were also taken into account with documentation of other potential developmental blockages. At index evaluation 66 out of the 100 met the criteria for recurrent depressive, dysthymic, cyclothymic, and bi-polar 2 disorders. 16 of those 66 showed signs of schizotypal personality. Other sub-groups included sociopathic, somatization, panic-agoraphobic, attention deficit, epileptic, and identity disorder. This in comparison to non-borderline personality controls faired significantly higher in risk for major affects excluding schizophrenic breakdowns during each of their follow-ups. As you can probably imagine prominent substance abuse history was evident as well as tempestuous biographies, and unstable early home environments were all common aspects. (The Authors. Journal of Child Pyschology and Psychiatry , 2015)

In contrast to an adult who takes 2 years in diagnosing with personality disorder, a child/adolescent only takes a year. The DSM-5 also tries to set criteria in identifying the disorder by stating: "the individual's particular maladaptive personality traits appear to be pervasive, persistent and unlikely to be limited to any particular span of development or contributing to another mental disorder", this sets the foundation in which the diagnosis can be applied.

- Abandonment fears
- Unstable and intense interpersonal relationships
- Identity disturbance
- Impulsivity
- Suicidal behavior
- Affective instability
- Chronic feelings of emptiness
- Inappropriate and intense anger with transient stress related paranoid ideation
- Severe disassociation symptoms

These are all signs of critique and symptoms of concern if noticed, and should be monitored within children/adolescent behavior. (World Health Organization, 1980). In addition, these same symptoms are created by the social construct of the culture as it further manipulates the norms of what is accepted and what is not...

What's wrong has been made right

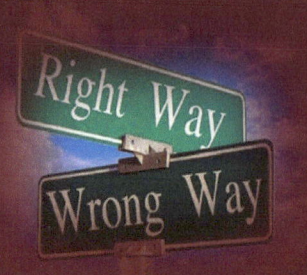

I personally believe right and wrong to be clearly defined, which eliminates the idea of a intersecting point giving them parallel paths...However the notion is something that I believe people try to capture by standing at this junction claiming neutrality. News is there's NO grey area, and the junction is a

Figure 6 Right & Wrong way

fabricated concept that ultimately leads people to more ease of doing wrong rather than the often struggle it takes to remain in the right way...

The Prophet Muhammad (saAllahu alaihi wasallam) said: "When Allah created Paradise, He said to Jibreel {Gabriel}: 'Go and look at it.' Jibreel went and looked at it, then came and said: 'O my Lord! By Thy might, no one who hears of it will fail to enter it.'

Allah then surrounded it with disagreeable things {Struggles, hardships, pain} and said: 'Go and look at it, Jibreel.' He went and looked at it, then came and said: 'O my Lord! By Thy might, I am afraid that no one will enter it.'

When Allah created Hell, He said: 'Go and look at it, Jibreel.' Jibreel went and looked at it, then came and said: 'O my Lord! By Thy might, no one who hears of it will enter it. '

Allah then surrounded it with desirable things {ease of doing wrong, the temping things meant to test who is sincere and who is not} and said: 'Go and look at it, Jibreel.' Jibreel went, looked at it, then came and said: 'O my Lord! By Thy might and power, I am afraid that no one will remain who does not enter it.' [Abu Dawud]

The reasons why Allah chose to surround each eternal dwelling with such things should be fairly easy to understand; for in this world when we work hard to achieve something we see ourselves more deserving of the reward verses those who don't...The same idea also holds true here. Tested with the bad and the good, because good is the incentive that often motivates people, but in order to test the sincerity of us all we are tested with the prohibited things as well.

For example: The most vivid with social, political and psychological effects in recent history is the de-classification of homosexuality. Separation of church from state was the successful effort of removing scriptural content from the influence of law and proper conduct of humanity in regards to his nature. Another huge milestone in Satan's plan was his lobbying of gay rights; activist who used the literature of man's law in the same mannerisms as minority groups had used the law in securing civil rights; copying the same principals of rights under the same term "Minority Group." But the ideas legislatively were born in Europe since the United States had largely kept to the illegality of homosexuality until the late 1960's early 70's. In 1553 England enacted the first secular law criminalizing homosexual practices making it punishable by hanging. The English colonies of America adapted English law against Sodomy citing the same scripture verse of:

Leviticus 20:13 **ASV**: (American Standard Version, 1901) *"And if a man lie with mankind, as with womankind, both of them have committed abomination: they shall surely be put to death; their blood shall be upon them."*

☐**KJV**: (King James Version): *"If a man also lie with mankind, as he lieth with a woman, both of them have committed an abomination: they shall surely be put to death. Their blood shall be upon them."*

The European decriminalization of sodomy began in post-Revolutionary France. The Constituent Assembly abrogated laws criminalizing "crimes against nature" in 1791 when it abolished ecclesiastical courts. This followed from the broader spirit of Enlightenment legal reform that protected the private sphere from state intrusion. The public and minors were still deemed to require state protection; therefore, the Law of 19-22 July 1791 and the Napoleonic Penal Code of 1810 criminalized "debauchery or corruption" of minors of either sex and "offenses against public decency" including sex in public places such as parks or bathrooms. However, the *Code Napoléon* never criminalized homosexuality itself thanks to the influence of Jean-Jacques-Régis de Cambacérès, the Second Consul who was a homosexual man. Men arrested under suspicion of public sex were subjected to medical examinations to help determine if anal sex had taken place. Therefore, medical-legal experts were the first to become interested in the scientific study of sexuality in the 19th century. (Association of Gay & Lesbian Psychiatrist , 2011).

German lawyer Karl Heinrich Ulrich's (1825-1895) was perhaps the first activist for homosexual civil rights. He argued against Germany's adoption of Prussian law criminalizing sodomy (Paragraph 175). In a series of pamphlets published from 1864 to 1879, he argued that same-sex love was a congenital, hereditary condition, not a matter of immorality; therefore, it should not be criminally persecuted. He called himself and those like him "Urgings" who had a female soul in a male body. He hypothesized that there were competing male and female "germs" that determined male and female anatomy and psyche (Association of Gay & Lesbian Psychiatrist , 2011). So, he himself was inclined toward the same misconduct. Adaptive & drawing from an historical transparency of prior bouts, activists began to utilize the same historical basis, reinvented for a new audience & culture. Once these simple rights were granted the criminalizing aspects of this heinous act was sought to be excused medically, then classifying it as a mental illness or some other tangent of gender dysphoria which was intended to water down the criminal perception. Daytime talk shows helped to popularize the idea as many publically spoke about their ordeals throughout childhood growing up in confused states of mind about their gender...

Empowerment changed Behavior

Up until 1974 Homosexuality was classified by the American Psychiatric Association as a mental illness one Sigmund Freud concluded to be inseparable from paranoia...Empowered socially & politically; activist began to come out of the closet in the early 1970's arguing against the classification of the APA, until by 1974 in the 7th edition of the DSM {Diagnostic Statistics Manual for Mental Disorders} removed the classification of homosexuality as a mental disorder/illness effectively paving its way to becoming a normality within society. With its removal came the stigma of sickness upon the majority who were against homosexual activity naming it homo-phobia which is a type of disorder. The mentally ill were now calling the normal sick effectively re-writing the societal norms of acceptance...

The decision was confirmed by a vote of the APA-membership with a vote of 13 to 0 with 2 abstentions... This action also helped to raise flags against the validity of all mental disorders and illnesses from a scientific perceptive, because if it was that easy to remove homosexuality from the DSM, then what was the scientific proof that gave it the classification in the first place? Concocted on the logic of human reasoning then on science that was less conclusive than it is today, seemed to have a fair footing of argument. But, on the basis of divine origin & our own nature is enough to refute any claim in argument. Even though throughout the ages this illicit act has sustained itself; its only because of the evil and chaos that it implants that has continued its lewdness. Sheer numbers of its participants in opposition to the punishments one was facing if caught doesn't give it appeal from deterministic viewpoint, nor does it help to highlight the indecency or refute the nature of our creation.

استِكْبَارًا فِي الْأَرْضِ وَمَكْرَ السَّيِّئِ ۚ وَلَا يَحِيقُ الْمَكْرُ السَّيِّئُ إِلَّا بِأَهْلِهِ ۚ فَهَلْ يَنظُرُونَ إِلَّا سُنَّتَ الْأَوَّلِينَ ۚ فَلَن تَجِدَ لِسُنَّتِ اللَّهِ تَبْدِيلًا ۖ وَلَن تَجِدَ لِسُنَّتِ اللَّهِ تَحْوِيلًا

[Due to] arrogance in the land and plotting of evil; but the evil plot does not encompass except its own people. Then do they await except the way of the former peoples? But you will never find in the way of Allah any change, and you will never find in the way of Allah any alteration. [Al-FaTir 35:43]

أَوَلَمْ يَسِيرُوا فِي الْأَرْضِ فَيَنْظُرُوا كَيْفَ كَانَ عَاقِبَةُ الَّذِينَ مِن قَبْلِهِمْ وَكَانُوا أَشَدَّ مِنْهُمْ قُوَّةً ۚ وَمَا كَانَ اللَّهُ لِيُعْجِزَهُ مِن شَيْءٍ فِي السَّمَاوَاتِ وَلَا فِي الْأَرْضِ ۚ إِنَّهُ كَانَ عَلِيمًا قَدِيرًا

Have they not traveled through the land and observed how was the end of those before them? And they were greater than them in power. But Allah is not to be caused failure by anything in the heavens or on the earth. Indeed, He is ever Knowing and Competent.[Al-FaTir 35:44]

The verses help to cement the fact that divine principal is forbearing and not changeable even when humanity seeks to plot against it in changing its application seeking to sow seeds of evil. Furthermore:

7:81 "Indeed you approach males in lust in place of women..."

اِنَّكُمْ لَتَأْتُونَ الرِّجَالَ شَهْوَةً مِّن دُونِ النِّسَاء

26:165-166 "What! Do you approach the males of the worlds and forsake those whom your Lord has created for you for your mates?"
Arabic: أَ تَأْتُونَ الذُّكْرَانَ مِنَ الْعَلَمِينَ ١ وَتَذَرُونَ مَا خَلَقَ لَكُمْ رَبُّكُم مِّنَ أَزْوَاجِكُمْ

27:55 "Will you indeed approach males in lust in place of women?"
Arabic: أَ ئِنَّكُمْ لَتَأْتُونَ الرِّجَالَ شَهْوَةً مِّنْ دُونِ النِّسَاءِ

29:28-29 "Most surely you are guilty of an indecency which none of the nations has ever done before you; What! do you come unto the males and cut the passageways [i.e. vas deferens and/or urethra] and commit evil in your clubs?"
Arabic: اِنَّكُمْ لَتَأْتُونَ الْفَاحِشَةَ مَا سَبَقَكُم بِهَا مِنْ أَحَدٍ مِّنَ الْعَلَمِينَ ١ أَ ئِنَّكُمْ لَتَأْتُونَ الرِّجَالَ وَتَقْطَعُونَ السَّبِيلَ وَتَأْتُونَ فِي نَادِيْكُمُ الْمُنْكَرَ

However, for the sake of science and from some of the usage I have seen of Ayat(s) in my research; I came across this website http://www.well.com/~aquarius/Qurannotes.htm. I found in it the author Mark Brustman, who also goes by the name Faris Malik, dissecting verses and language to adapt homosexual tafsir (explanation) of Quran {A'oothu bi'llah min tha'lik}. For example:

لَّهِ مُلْكُ السَّمَاوَاتِ وَالْأَرْضِ ۚ يَخْلُقُ مَا يَشَاءُ ۚ يَهَبُ لِمَن يَشَاءُ إِنَاثًا وَيَهَبُ لِمَن يَشَاءُ الذُّكُورَ

To Allah belongs the dominion of the heavens and the earth; He creates what he wills. He gives to whom He wills female [children], and He gives to whom He wills males.[Ash-Shura 42:49]

أَوْ يُزَوِّجُهُمْ ذُكْرَانًا وَإِنَاثًا ۖ وَيَجْعَلُ مَن يَشَاءُ **عَقِيمًا** ۚ إِنَّهُ عَلِيمٌ قَدِيرٌ

Or He makes them [both] males and females, and He renders whom He wills **barren**. Indeed, He is Knowing and Competent. [Ash-Shura 42:50]

The highlighted word in Arabic is A'qeeman, which means Barren {which in the verse here further means they don't have the ability} because this is the condition on those whom Allah wills. So, let's examine the two verses a bit further to see where they stray off course in the exegesis of the Quran in making their desires acceptable through scripture...

1. Allah first states his dominion {power & rule over all the heavens and earth} لَّهِ مُلْكُ السَّمَاوَاتِ وَالْأَرْضِ
2. He states that it is he who creates as he wills يَخْلُقُ مَا يَشَاءُ
3. And bestows on whom he wills يَهَبُ لِمَن يَشَاءُ from that bestowment إِنَاثًا females وَيَهَبُ لِمَن يَشَاءُ الذُّكُورَ and he bestows also on who he wills males...
4. OR...أَوْ يُزَوِّجُهُمْ **He combines them**...this is the misinterpretation and the word that leads them to deviate especially in English translation...This doesn't mean both the feminine and masculine in one as gay or homosexuals might conclude...

أَوْ يُزَوِّجُهُمْ This word in English sounds like "yu'zaw'wee'ju'hum." The prefix "yu" his referring to Allah and the ending "hum" means "them"...This leaves the sarf {root} of the word "zaw'wej" which is the gender neutral term for spouse. This word is also use in connection to creation meaning "pair"...

يَا أَيُّهَا النَّاسُ اتَّقُوا رَبَّكُمُ الَّذِي خَلَقَكُم مِّن نَّفْسٍ وَاحِدَةٍ وَخَلَقَ مِنْهَا زَوْجَهَا وَبَثَّ مِنْهُمَا رِجَالًا كَثِيرًا وَنِسَاءً ۚ وَاتَّقُوا اللَّهَ الَّذِي تَسَاءَلُونَ بِهِ وَالْأَرْحَامَ ۚ إِنَّ اللَّهَ كَانَ عَلَيْكُمْ رَقِيبًا

O mankind, fear your Lord, who created you from one soul and created from it its mate and dispersed from both of them many men and women. And fear Allah, through whom you ask one another, and the wombs. Indeed Allah is ever, over you, an Observer. [An'Nisa 4:1]

- وَخَلَقَ مِنْهَا Allah says he created one soul {Adam} خَلَقَكُم مِّن نَّفْسٍ وَاحِدَةٍ and then from him his mate {spouse Eve} زَوْجَهَا and from the وَبَثَّ مِنْهُمَا رِجَالاً كَثِيراً وَنِسَاءً two of them raised many men & women {all the succeeding generations of human-being}. This verse is sufficient in deducing the false claim of homosexuality. For زوج zawj in the context of the verse meant the pairing of creation Adam and from him the woman Hawah {eve}.

عن أبي عبد الرحمن عبد الله بن مسعود رضي الله عنه ، قال : حدثنا رسول الله صلي الله عليه وسلم – وهو الصادق إن أحدكم يجمع خلقه في بطن أمه أربعين يوما نطفه ، ثم يكون علقة مثل ذلك ، ثم يكون مضغة) : –المصدوق مثل ذلك ، ثم يرسل إليه الملك ، فينفخ فيه الروح ، ويؤمر بأربع كلمات : بكتب رزقه ، واجله ، وعمله ، وشقي أم سعيد ؛ فوالله الذي لا إله غيره إن أحدكم ليعمل بعمل أهل الجنه حتى ما يكون بينه وبينها إلا ذراع فيسبق عليه وإن أحدكم ليعمل بعمل أهل النار حتي ما يكون بينه وبينها إلا ذراع الكتاب فيعمل بعمل أهل النار فيدخلها [ومسلم [رقم : 2643 [3208 : فـيسبق عليه الكتاب فيعمل بعمل أهل الجنة فيدخلها) رواه البخاري [رقم

On the authority of Aboo `Abd ir-Rahmaan `Abdullaah ibn Mas`ood (radiAllaahu anhu), who said: The Messenger of Allaah (sallAllaahu alayhi wa sallam) and he is the Truthful, the Believed, narrated to us:

Verily the creation of each one of you is brought together in his mother's womb for forty days in the form of a nutfah (a drop), then he becomes an 'alaqah (clot of blood) for a like period, then a mudghah (morsel of flesh) for a like period, then there is sent to him the angel who blows his soul into him and the angel says, "O Allah male or female", then the angel told the gender; The angel is then commanded with four matters: to write down his Rizq (sustenance), his life span, his actions, and whether he will be happy or unhappy (i.e. whether or not he will enter Paradise). {All of these matters are all within the encompassing knowledge of Allah}.

[Narrated by al-Bukhaari (البخاري) and Muslim (صحيح مسلم).]

This is why some jurists agreed on the **need** of abortion {when there is a medical excuse}, not in general, but when it is needed there is no harm, because the spirit has not yet been breathed in...One last open ended question remains, and that is, "What about inter-sexual"? Those born with both female & male genitalia...Well, for a transsexual woman (assigned male at birth), genital surgery generally gives her a functional vagina constructed from her prior genitalia. It does not, however, give her ovaries, a uterus or a cervix. Medical science is far from being able to transplant those female reproductive organs for anyone, trans or not. For a transsexual man (assigned female at birth), genital surgery generally gives him male genitalia that can sometimes be used for sex. It does not, however, give him functional testicles, and doctors are far from perfecting transplants for them, too. (Herman, 2011).

 This medical understanding doesn't contradict the gender assignment of the person, but helps to re-confirm it as its predominant nature. Congenital adrenal hyperplasia is another genetic cause of transgender. Worth mentioning is that epigenetic effects can be passed on just like genetic effects. Therefore, this condition would be more so classified as a genetic mutation, and the right follow up action after medical determination of the child would be critical for proper psychological development avoiding gender confusion. It shouldn't be considered a choice of the individual who didn't create him/herself...and should be the responsibility of the parent to prevent the need of psychological treatment in the future...

This has been the plot of Satan working through man and the homosexual revolution of the 1970's opened the door to the sexual revolution & hyper-sexualized society of today. With that has come every other kind of corruption in accompaniment. That's because sexual immorality of a society is the last standing defense of its overall modesty. In turn, the driven lustful states of mind propagated by media & advertisement perpetuate a virtual, fantasy world within our individual spaces of times that captures the lowly desires of mankind through our natural inclinations and compulsion.

The Prophet s.a.w said, " By the One, other than Whom there is no deity, verily one of you performs the actions of the people of Paradise until there is but an arm's length between him and it, and that which has been written overtakes him, and so he acts with the actions of the people of the Hellfire and thus enters it; and verily one of you performs the actions of the people of the Hellfire, until there is but an arm's length between him and it, and that which has been written overtakes him and so he acts with the actions of the people of Paradise and thus he enters it..." [Narrated by al-Bukhaari (البخاري) and Muslim (مسلم) (صحيح مسلم).]

Ideal vs Real self

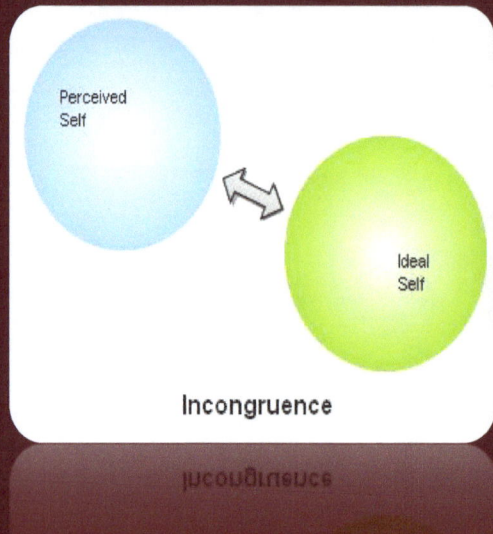

Figure 7 the self in-congruence

One of the symptoms to BPD {borderline personality disorder} is the identity crises. In terms of the previous topic of transgender the reality is that we don't have good statistics. We don't have a census question, or set of questions about people in the household who may have gender incongruence. And the numbers really vary widely. For example, the numbers that are derived from Western clinics about the prevalence of this, say about 1 in 30K male-bodied people have a female gender identity and one in 100K female-bodied people have a male gender identity. But these statistics come from clinics where people are seeking care specifically seeking sexual reassignment surgeries, and for many reasons, those are very low numbers, and they are probably very, inaccurately reflect how often this happens. {*Johanna Olson, MD Medical Director, Center for Transyouth Health and Development, Children's hospital Los Angeles*}. The self-actualising tendency is our striving to have the real-self match with our version of ideal-self. The figure above shows the two spheres moving away from each other like common-poled magnets which resist one another. Positive self-regard & self-esteem that is either conditional or unconditional direct us in evaluating ourselves in worthiness. When our evaluation is set on conditions such as what others expect or prefer then our ideal-self might be something far off from the real-self. Living a lie, a phrase that is often used in explaining this concept...

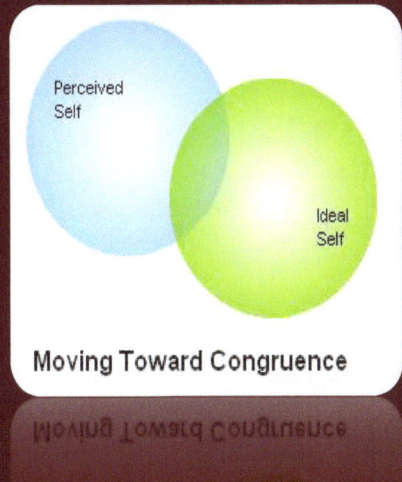

Moving Toward Congruence

On the other side of those conditions that affect our congruence is the path of direction which allows fulfillment... Open experiences, trust of one's self, confidence all of what make the human-being more complete. This of course cannot take place only with psychological, intellectual & physical development...This concept also has to be in line with the spiritual. {Refer to volume 1 again on the principals of the spirit & heart}

Since the human organism is made of dual natures both have to be congruent in order for harmony to be present. In fact, the best way of viewing both these models is to see the spirit {our pure selves} as the "Ideal-self" and the 'Real-self" as the perceived self. This should be an easier way of understanding this since we have all made at one time or another a self-inventory, of which should be an ongoing thing.

Whenever I present these ideas or models I tend to focus the data on the adolescent group because these will be the adults of tomorrow. Furthermore this self-concept of realization seems to be heavily effecting our youth today in designation to blind groupings & confusion of many young people resulting in addictions, pre-marital sex/pregnancy, mood disorders, anger, failing education, and often suicide. Public relations officials who design the interface of society with its populace very discretely attack the self-identity through a variety of campaigns all aimed at redirecting and reshaping society's perceptions of culture. This crisis within the self is not only one of the early symptoms to BPD {border-line personality disorder} it also plays host to a mirage of potential other negative illness and or problems. Our identities are both personal & social; which we showcase one and limit the other towards social & group audiences.

- Social= ability to interact with others
- Competence- ability to meet basic needs
- Affect= awareness of emotional states
- Physical= feelings about looks, health, physical condition, and overall appearance.
- Academic= Success or failure in school
- Family= how well one functions within the family unit

Each of these plays into the overall psyche and forming the concepts by which we formulate our self-worthiness. Again, the pressures of a more competitive society vs cooperative place tremendous stresses on adolescence causing many to fail in the actualization of self. In addition, environment, social status & genetic constructs further the potential causes of mental illnesses that affect our personalities.

Nurturing Iman in our children

Television programming is literally re-writing the ways in which people interact and carry out life, as T.V. is used through its entertainment factor to prescribe culture. As society continues to tug on the souls of people by turning them in-side out in retrospect of true reality and self, the sicknesses of society will only deepen. Disturbing the natural harmony of the human-being {Al-fitrah} and then subjecting it to mechanisms designed to further misguide it, the personality and identity of the person(s) will be extremely vulnerable to mental disorder.

Unless...We refocus our attention & efforts on restoring the concept of faith in our children; by that I don't mean by stating merely the vague concepts to belief and practices. Instead, we must educate them on the whys, providing them with answers to their questions, and instilling within them the love of faith: Allah, his prophet(s), his Angels, books, Jannah, Jahannam, and Qadr-ul-Allah...

From the conversation Musa a.s. {Moses} was having with Firaun {pharaoh} when he was regarding himself a god, Musa a.s. responds to his questioning:

قَالَ فَمَن رَّبُّكُمَا يَا مُوسَىٰ

[Pharaoh] said, "So who is the Lord of you two, O Moses?" [Ta-Ha 20:49]

قَالَ رَبُّنَا الَّذِي أَعْطَىٰ كُلَّ شَيْءٍ خَلْقَهُ ثُمَّ هَدَىٰ

He said, "Our Lord is He who gave each thing its form and then guided [it]."[Ta-Ha 20:50]

So, we can see through the inspiration of Musa a.s. in his conversation with Firaun, that Allah creates, gives everything its shape/form and then guides it...This guidance for the creation is the "wahy" {swift transmission of information; here regarding its inherent instincts or divine decree or physical principals of laws} for example the sun, moon, stars etc. have governing principals by which they follow for their prescribed term which never changes. Plant life, and the animal kingdom all follow their inherent instinctual given guidance. All of such things {creation excluding mankind & Jinn} are in complete submission to its design and purpose something that the human being & Jinn have to choose. When we submit to our creators limits and obey his wishes through his divine scripture {wahy also refers to revelation, & divine inspiration} and the Human/Jinn is then rightly guided to the best life in this world and the one to come.

وَمَن يُطِعِ اللَّهَ وَالرَّسُولَ فَأُولَٰئِكَ مَعَ الَّذِينَ أَنْعَمَ اللَّهُ عَلَيْهِم مِّنَ النَّبِيِّينَ وَالصِّدِّيقِينَ وَالشُّهَدَاءِ وَالصَّالِحِينَ ۚ وَحَسُنَ أُولَٰئِكَ رَفِيقًا

And whoever obeys Allah and the Messenger - those will be with the ones upon whom Allah has bestowed favor of the prophets, the steadfast affirmers of truth, the martyrs and the righteous. And excellent are those as companions.[An-Nisa 4:69]

After all, personality is the uniqueness of our emotional, behavioral & cognitive characteristics that distinguish us as individuals; from these characteristics we form our identity that becomes our own self-perception that is then put forth into society.

Maturity (Islam vs Western)

In the west, adolescent youth conduct themselves like adults in many ways and rightfully so after attaining puberty; however Western culture is still within the mindset of treating them like children until the ages of 18 to 21 years. In contrast to many countries here in Africa, it's not uncommon to see a 4 or 5yr girl/boy walking to the store for their parents or carrying out some other duty that they are physically or mentally able to perform. Childhood is therefore much shorter in these areas in terms of being non-responsible...this of course doesn't mean that all of the playing & games seize; on the contrary they're responsibilities are shared with times of play. Children then seem to have a better correlating mesh between biology and responsibility in terms of young-adulthood and treated as such. Many western views, maybe even some from yourselves might suggest what about the maturity of the child? Western viewpoints tend to couple maturity with age only limiting children to a collective intelligence that can't exceed their years on earth.

This drastically strains the mental development of intelligence in contrast to the biological maturity that has been reached. This concept of maturity then is directly proportional to the cultural viewpoints working in contrast to the psyche & physiological design of our complete development culminating at puberty. In Islam and much of the Eastern world view, the attainment of puberty marks the mandate of adulthood. In these years mental & physical strength peak; while there is still more learned ability ongoing through middle-adulthood our strengths are much earlier on. It is in fact this ignorance and or deliberate change in view-point that harms individual development in countries like America. This is one of the reasons why I believe & we see much of the bad behavior continued on into the 20's of many of the youth because they have been treated in lesser capacities far longer than they should.

While the Prophet Muhammad s.a.w. was making the call to Islam, he received a large part of his support from youth who comprised the social segment that was open to new things, idealist and energetic. In fact, while several of the first Muslims were around 50 years-old and several were above 35, the age of the remaining majority was under thirty.

For example, the age of the following persons who accepted Islam at an early age was:

- Ali Ibn Abi Talib (ra) 10
- Abdullah ibn Umar & Ubayda ibn al-Jarrah 13,
- Uqba ibn Amir 14
- Jabir ibn Abdullah and Zayd ibn Harise 15
- Abdullah ibn Mas'ud, Habbab ibn Aret and Zubayr ibn Awwam 16
- Talha ibn Ubaydullah, Abdurrahman ibn Awf, Arkam ibn Abi'l-Arkam, Sa'd Ibn Abi Wakkas and Asma bint Abu Bakr 17
- Muaz Ibn Jabel and Mus'ab Ibn Umayr 18
- Abu Musa al-Ash'ari 19
- Jafir Ibn Abu Talib 22
- Osman Ibn Huwayris, Osman Ibn Affan, Abu Ubayda, Abu Hurayra and Umar 25-31 (Bunyamin Erul, 2010)

This has always been the response to social inequality & revolutionary change; the response of the youth has always being the closet to Islam, ready to usher in change that the older populations have grown adept too and more inclined to resist any changes.

Our youth are the target of intellectual crimes both from an educational bias as well as from a societal limitation imposed on them in their reduced status of adulthood in treatment. Children are otherwise encouraged to carry on in adult like fashion with pre-marital relationships, beauty pageants for the very young in full make up and revealing clothing, sex, pregnancy, work, loans/credit, and even take up legal actions against their own parents...but they ARE NOT so encouraged in ways of adult responsibilities or with efforts of enhancing their intellectual levels.

Mental deficiency from a secularized view has been commonly linked to:

- Poverty- Low IQ is a strong precursor to poverty, more so than socio economic factors like where people grow up.
- Schooling- dropping out of school before the completion of high school
- Unemployment, idleness, or injury
- Family Matters
- Welfare dependency
- Parenting
- Crime
- Civility and Citizenship

These particular conditions do play their roles in impacting our intelligence, but they aren't the absolute conditions that determine intelligence. Actually it's the viewpoint itself that creates such symptoms within society in the first place. So, it's a shame that a society would therefore create a situation and in turn use subsequent consequences that they latter pass blame too rather than to the initial source cause… In addition to general intelligence coined the "g-factor" by Charles Spearman (1863-1945); Howard Gardner (1983-1999) proposed the idea of multiple intelligences. He suggested this was an evolutionary function that would vary among different people intrinsically infused with our talents and developed skill sets.

Unless otherwise tested for specific intelligence the general factor is usually the basis of the test. The following graph suggests the global intelligence…

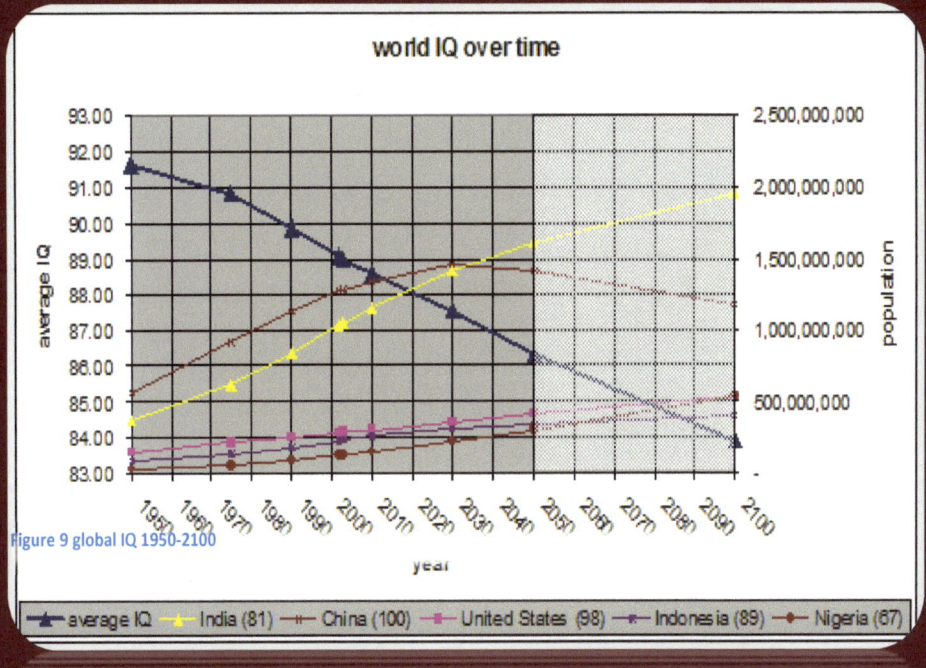

Figure 9 global IQ 1950-2100

The larger the human population grows the average human IQ seems to drop. I might suggest that one factor that leads to the overall lowering of IQ points globally is the inclusion of America into the equation. One such reason is America has consistently fallen academically to lower and lower world ranking... Since the 1950's the IQ average has dropped 3pts; however most people fall between the ranges of 89 to 100 which is the global norm. (William McConochie, 2010). Anything below 89 would be considered below standard with anything below 70 would then begin to fall into the mentally retardation levels. On the higher end of the scale above 100 would be exceptional while 115 an above would be the gifted level. For what it's worth cultural biases and problems with standardization still pose problems in collecting better accuracy. Education and the way its structured is actually impeding success of our children rather than enhancing it. The entire system is based on a competitive standard that is often very stressful on students.

- Grading {research proves that kids tend to lose interest in the learning itself and focus more on the means of getting a passing grade rather than engage into the lesson, because they tend to think less deeply about the lesson the retain-ment of the subject matter is lessened, as a result children will often pick the easiest task because it seems to be something that will maximize obtaining that goal and not necessarily due to laziness...
- Where applicable, Memorization of prior concepts only without encouraging deeper thinking in discovery of newer ideas and hidden wisdoms.
- Standardization of test which are then collectively compared to individuals in the same age groups that compare rather than measure intelligence. Some of the deepest thinking people, just don't do well on test.

intelligence encompasses much more than generalized knowledge. Human beings are born with a variety of divinely bestowed gifts and each of us develops differently prior to neuro-pruning of puberty where millions of unused neuro transmitters are cut away...

Prior to this process of pruning, those of use that were fortunate to have parents who kept our minds aroused with different mental & physical tasks are able to see the manifestations of those efforts in our developed skills and talents...Those most publicized are the sports or musical Phenom's that verily easily excel more so than the older persons who share the same craft. Gardener defines these additional intelligences in eight different categories.

The multiple intelligence models tend to be influential in the educational fields.

1. Linguistic-the ability to speak, read and write well
2. Logic-mathematical- the ability to use logic an mathematical skills to solve problems
3. Spatial- ability to think and reason about objects in 3-dimensional
4. Musical- ability to perform and enjoy music
5. Kinesthetic- ability to move the body in sports or other physical activity

6. Interpersonal- ability to understand and interact effectively with others.
7. Intrapersonal- ability to have insight into the self
8. Naturalistic- ability to recognise, identifies, and understands animals, plants, and other living things...

This list of intelligences is often criticized as abilities rather than intelligences; nonetheless ability shouldn't be misunderstood as something separate from intelligence but rather they are in fact inter-related and interdependent working in tandem. I believe one reason for this misunderstanding is due to the ignorance of humanities dual nature again as already previously stated. The body is an organism that is merged with the spirit, and by that it is easy to see that knowledge resides with the spiritual portion; while the spiritual presence gives utilization to mental ability that in turn gives enabled action to the physical body. The body and all of its complex architecture give us our physical movement and presence in the world. If you conceptualize this idea, it's easy to see our alienation to the world we live, through our created vessels give us to reside temporarily before returning back to the source of our creation. Disbelief for me in regards to human science is something quite arrogant, because it really does take arrogance to remain in disbelief...

Ibn Taymimah {rahimuallah} was once quoted in saying, "The Spirit {ruh} floats through the body"; it isn't something fixed. This statement is in agreeance with the statements of the prophet about the extraction of the soul disbeliever and believer: *"But when the unbelieving servant is leaving this world and going onto the Hereafter, angels with dark faces descend upon him, with them are coarse sack-cloth, and they sit at a distance from him as far as the eye can see. Then the Angel of Death comes and sits by his head and says," O foul soul, come out to Allah's displeasure and anger."* **So the soul spreads throughout his body,** *{It is not in the same shape as our human form, Not wanting to come out}* *so he drags it out just as a pronged roasting fork is pulled through wool. So he takes it, but just as a pronged roasting fork is pulled through wool. So he takes it, but does not leave it in his hand for the blink of an eye until they put it in those coarse sack-cloths. Then there comes from him an offensive stench like that of the foulest smelling corpse rotting upon the face of the earth. Than the prophet (S.A.W.) continued," So they ascend with it (i.e. the soul) and they do not pass by and group of angels except that they say, "What is this foul smell?" So they say, "So and so, son of so and so," calling him with the ugliest names which he used to be called with in this world, until they come with him to the lowest heaven and ask for permission to enter, and it is not opened for him."* Then Allah's Messenger (S.A.W.) recited (verse 40 from *Surat Al-'Araf*):

إِنَّ الَّذِينَ كَذَّبُوا بِآيَاتِنَا وَاسْتَكْبَرُوا عَنْهَا لَا تُفَتَّحُ لَهُمْ أَبْوَابُ السَّمَاءِ وَلَا يَدْخُلُونَ الْجَنَّةَ حَتَّى يَلِجَ الْجَمَلُ فِي سَمِّ الْخِيَاطِ ۚ وَكَذَٰلِكَ نَجْزِي الْمُجْرِمِينَ

Indeed, those who deny Our verses and are arrogant toward them - the gates of Heaven will not be opened for them, nor will they enter Paradise until a camel enters into the eye of a needle. And thus do We recompense the criminals. (Which is impossible)**."** And the prophet (S.A.W.) continued, *"Allah, the Mighty and Magnificent, says, "Write his record in (Sejjeen) within the lowest earth." Then his soul is flung down,* and then Allah's Messenger (S.A.W.) recited (verse 31 from *Surat* Al-Hajj):

حُنَفَاءَ لِلّهِ غَيْرَ مُشْرِكِينَ بِهِ ۚ وَمَن يُشْرِكْ بِاللّهِ فَكَأَنَّمَا خَرَّ مِنَ السَّمَاءِ فَتَخْطَفُهُ الطَّيْرُ أَوْ تَهْوِي بِهِ الرِّيحُ فِي مَكَانٍ سَحِيقٍ

Inclining [only] to Allah, not associating [anything] with Him. And he who associates with Allah - it is as though he had fallen from the sky and was snatched by the birds or the wind carried him down into a remote place. The prophet (S.A.W.) continued, *"So his soul is returned to his body and two angels come and make him sit up. Then they will say to him, "Who is your Lord?" So He will say, "Ah, Ah, I do not know." So they will say to him, "What is your Deen?" SO he will say, "Ah, Ah, I do not know." So they will say to him, "Who is this man who was sent amongst you?" So he will say, "Ah, Ah, I do not know." So a caller will call from heaven, "You have lied so spread a place for him in the Fire, and open a door to the Fire for him." So some of its heat and scorching air comes upon him, and his grave is constricted to the extent that his ribs interlace…*

The prophet (S.A.W.) continued, *"A man with an ugly face, unsightly clothes and smelling offensively comes to him and says, "Receive news of that which will grieve you, this is the day which you were promised." So he will say, "Who are you? Your face is ugly and seems to signify evil. "So he will say, "I am your evil deeds." So he will say, "O May Lord, Do not establish the Last Hour."{The punishment serves to be both psychological and physical which the spirit embodies both}.*

As for the believer: "When the Believing servant is leaving this world and going on to the Hereafter, angels with bright faces -as if their faces were the sun - descend upon him. With them is a shroud from Paradise and perfume for embalming from the perfume of Paradise, so they sit away from him at the distance the eye can see and then the Angel of Death, (A.S.) comes and sits by his head and says, "O good soul, come out to forgiveness from Allah and His good pleasure." He said, "So it comes out (smoothly) just as a drop flows out from the mouth of the drinking vessel, and he takes it, but does not leave it in his hand even for the blink of an eye until they take it and place it in that shroud and that perfume, and there comes out from him a smell like that of the best musk found upon the face of the earth."

Then the prophet (S.A.W.) continued, *"So they ascend with it [i.e. the person's soul] and they do not pass by any group of the angels except that they say, "Who is this good and pure soul?" So they reply, "So and so, son of so and so," with the best of his names which he used to be called by in this world until they come with him to the lowest heaven and ask that it be opened for him, so it is opened for him, so they accompany him through every heaven to the next one until he is taken up to the seventh heaven, and Allah, the Mighty and Magnificent, says, "Write the record of my servant in "Elliyyoon (which is the place of the books of the believers. And Allah continues; return the soul to the earth to his body." So then two angels come to him and make him sit up. Then they say, "Who is your Lord?" So he will say, "My Lord is Allah." So they say, "what is your Deen (religion)?' So he will say, "My Deen is Islam." So they say, "Who is this man who was sent amongst you?" So he will say, "He is Allah's Messenger." So they say, "How did you come to know that?" So he will say," I read the Book of Allah, and believed in it and attested to it." So a caller will call from heaven, "Indeed my servant has spoken the truth, so spread a place for him in Paradise, and open a door to Paradise for him." He said, "So some of its fragrance and scent comes to him and his grave is extended as far as the eye can see."*

Then the prophet (S.A.W.) continued," A person with a handsome face, beautiful clothes and good smell comes to him and says, "Receive good news which will please you. This is the day which you were promised." So he says to him, "Who are you? Since your face appears to signify good/well." So he says. "I am you righteous deeds." He therefore says, "O may Lord, establish the Last Hour, O may Lord establish the Last Hour- so that I may return to my family and wealth."

It is further understood that the brain is mere a tool that develops neuro-logically, organically, chemically & physically, but carries on with its development throughout our interactions with the outside world and our mental arousals that solidify left and right brain path ways etc….The brain is therefore a mechanism that gives the spirit interpretation of how we learn, remember, problem-solve, and pay attention to our surrounding world(s) and these concepts aren't based on any knowledge. The brain is the process center for the spirit to interact in its new world. For example: when the telephone rings answering it doesn't require any knowledge; instead it requires perceptional/auditory intelligence of recognition of what a phone is & hearing the phone ring, decision making {to answer it or not}, motor skills kinetic {to lift the receiver}, linguistic {language and speaking to understand & be understood}, interpersonal {skills to interpret tone of voice to interact properly with another human being}. These cognitive abilities {of Gardner's model} are supported by neural networks that I mentioned develop until pruning occurs at puberty.

This early building of our cognitive abilities strengthens our abilities, but these abilities are further divided into mental ability & physical ability. Mental abilities can limit physical ability, but physical ability isn't a normal condition that inhibits mental ability…For example: the very famous theoretical Physicist Steven Hawking is completely paralyzed and speaks through a computer, but his physical ability isn't something that inhibits his mental functioning…However, lack of physical activity can make a person mentally lazy… Thus understanding intelligence requires that we understand the norms of the population at each respective age typically determined by this equation: [IQ=mental age/chronological age * 100]

Chronological age that isn't evenly matched or exceeding the mental age is cause for alarm, but more importantly should be something focused on in prevention since much of the early brain development once lost from non-utilization makes it much more difficult later to learn.

وَهُوَ الَّذِي مَدَّ الْأَرْضَ وَجَعَلَ فِيهَا رَوَاسِيَ وَأَنْهَارًا ۖ وَمِن كُلِّ الثَّمَرَاتِ جَعَلَ فِيهَا زَوْجَيْنِ اثْنَيْنِ ۖ يُغْشِي اللَّيْلَ النَّهَارَ ۚ إِنَّ فِي ذَٰلِكَ لَآيَاتٍ لِّقَوْمٍ يَتَفَكَّرُونَ

And it is He who spread the earth and placed therein firmly set mountains and rivers; and from all of the fruits He made therein two mates {the seed and egg of reproduction}; He causes the night to cover the day. Indeed in that are signs for a people who give thought... [Al-A'rad 13:3]

وَفِي الْأَرْضِ قِطَعٌ مُّتَجَاوِرَاتٌ وَجَنَّاتٌ مِّنْ أَعْنَابٍ وَزَرْعٌ وَنَخِيلٌ صِنْوَانٌ وَغَيْرُ صِنْوَانٍ يُسْقَىٰ بِمَاءٍ وَاحِدٍ وَنُفَضِّلُ بَعْضَهَا عَلَىٰ بَعْضٍ فِي الْأُكُلِ ۚ إِنَّ فِي ذَٰلِكَ لَآيَاتٍ لِّقَوْمٍ يَعْقِلُونَ

And within the land are neighboring plots and gardens of grapevines and crops and palm trees, [growing] several from a root or otherwise, watered with one water; but We make some of them exceed others in [quality of] fruit. Indeed in that are signs for a people who reason. [Al-A'rad 13:4]

The Quran encourages reason and our contemplation over the words of the almighty in showing us of his signs. Intelligence is something of great importance for it elevates the human being above the animal creation. So, what is the difference between Wisdom & Intelligence? It's said that intelligence is primarily that for present life, giving us our primary function and interaction in daily life, but wisdom is something of much higher order in enabling human nature and good judgement in important or uncertain matters of life. "Intelligence enabled people to build a nuclear bomb; Wisdom makes them consider the stupidity of do so in the first place..." It is thereby forbidden to harm the development or conscious state of the mind with poor parenting, Alcohol, witch craft {magic of all kinds}, superstition, deceitful philosophy & blind following...So, intelligence is also said to having a shifting line one that can lean more toward stupidity when we consider some of our behaviors.

Trying to bridge the gap between our early predecessors and their ways of growing intellectually with our conditions of today, we must see the importance of transferring that intelligence into the acquisition of knowledge but, how do we do that? Well, it's easy if you've contemplated over the last few pages...the human is dual natured {body/spirit} and the body needs intelligence to operate and function in daily life with it host of tasks, but the spirit is not enhanced by worldly intelligence; on the contrary it requires that of a spiritual source in order to grow. This is the limitation of secular knowledge because it serves only one aspect of the human being discounting his/her totality...This is also the premise that gives rise to many failed and unanswered societal problems. Secular knowledge lacks wisdom, and focuses on the present, not future outcomes of choices or decisions made today.

Spiritual Intelligence

- Is the ability to transcend
- Ability to enter heightened states of consciousness
- Ability to invest everyday activities, events, and relationships with a sense of the sacred, which means through religious knowledge everything becomes worship...
- Ability to use spiritual resources to solve problems in living.
- And engage in virtuous behavior...

وَأَمَّا الَّذِينَ كَفَرُوا أَفَلَمْ تَكُنْ آيَاتِي تُتْلَى عَلَيْكُمْ فَاسْتَكْبَرْتُمْ وَكُنتُمْ قَوْمًا مُّجْرِمِينَ

But as for those who disbelieved, [it will be said], "Were not Our verses recited to you, but you were arrogant {because they thought secular knowledge was sufficient} and became a people of criminals? {meaning disbelievers who acted outside divine law} { [Al-Jathiya 45:31]

وَإِذَا قِيلَ إِنَّ وَعْدَ اللَّهِ حَقٌّ وَالسَّاعَةُ لَا رَيْبَ فِيهَا قُلْتُم مَّا نَدْرِي مَا السَّاعَةُ إِن نَّظُنُّ إِلَّا ظَنًّا وَمَا نَحْنُ بِمُسْتَيْقِنِينَ

And when it was said, 'Indeed, the promise of Allah is truth and the Hour [is coming] {secular knowledge doesn't remind us of the coming hour} - no doubt about it,' you said, 'We know not what is the Hour. We assume only assumption, and we are not convinced.' " [Al-Jathiya 45:32]

وَبَدَا لَهُمْ سَيِّئَاتُ مَا عَمِلُوا وَحَاقَ بِهِم مَّا كَانُوا بِهِ يَسْتَهْزِئُونَ

And the evil consequences of what they did will appear to them, and they will be enveloped by what they used to ridicule. [Al-Jathiya 45:33]

وَقِيلَ الْيَوْمَ نَنسَاكُمْ كَمَا نَسِيتُمْ لِقَاء يَوْمِكُمْ هَٰذَا وَمَأْوَاكُمُ النَّارُ وَمَا لَكُم مِّن نَّاصِرِينَ

And it will be said, "Today We will forget you as you forgot the meeting of this Day of yours, and your refuge is the Fire, and for you there are no helpers. {Al-Jathiya 45:34]

ذَٰلِكُم بِأَنَّكُمُ اتَّخَذْتُمْ آيَاتِ اللهِ هُزُوًا وَغَرَّتْكُمُ الْحَيَاةُ الدُّنْيَا ۚ فَالْيَوْمَ لَا يُخْرَجُونَ مِنْهَا وَلَا هُمْ يُسْتَعْتَبُونَ

That is because you took the verses of Allah in ridicule, and worldly life deluded you." So that Day they will not be removed from it, nor will they be asked to appease [Allah]. [Al-Jathiya 45:35]

فَلِلَّهِ الْحَمْدُ رَبِّ السَّمَاوَاتِ وَرَبِّ الْأَرْضِ رَبِّ الْعَالَمِينَ

Then, to Allah belongs [all] praise - Lord of the heavens and Lord of the earth, Lord of the worlds. [Al-Jathiya 45:36]

وَلَهُ الْكِبْرِيَاءُ فِي السَّمَاوَاتِ وَالْأَرْضِ ۖ وَهُوَ الْعَزِيزُ الْحَكِيمُ

And to Him belongs [all] grandeur within the heavens and the earth, and He is the Exalted in Might, the Wise. [Al-Jathiya 45:37]

Young sahaba (ra) {Companions of Prophet (saw)}

In comparison to Gardner's 8 identifying categories of intelligence, I find it somewhat similar to the definitions behind the 13 found in the study of Arabic language which is used to study Quran and other sciences of scripture...

The Sciences of the Arabic Language are composed of 13 different sciences:

1) Morphology الصّرْف
2) Grammar الإعراب (which goes under the term النَّحْو)
3) Writing الرَّسْم أو الإملاء
4) Meanings المعاني

5) Science which deals which metaphorical language البيان
6) The Art of beautiful style البديع
7) Metrics or Prosody العروض
8) Rhyme القوافي
9) Writing Poetry قَرْضُ الشَّعِر
10) Composition الإنْشاء
11) Public Speech and Oration الخطابة
12) Literary History تاريخُ اللأدب
13) Core of the Arabic Language مَتن اللُّغة (deals with words, foundations, dictionaries, and lexicons) Some scholars group البديع و البيان و المعاني under the Science of Arabic Rhetoric (علمُ البَلاغة)

Students who have been introduced to the memorization of Quran and its sciences along with the study of Hadith, tafsir, fiqh etc.; have all faired far better at the time of entry into secular systems of education. The reason behind this concept is the Quran like other previous scriptures (In their true contents which are today lost) were divine sources of ultimate truth that when studied allowed mankind the opportunity to understanding his/her world better through the words of the one who created all things, as well as the sciences that surround their governing principals, and laws of existence.

As reported by Anas b. Malik, there were 70 youth from the Ansari and they called themselves the "Qurra." In the evening they would disperse into various districts of Medina and form lesson groups. They would lead the people in prayer and return to the Prophet's masjid in the morning. On one particular occasion the Prophet (saw)

Islam & Mathematics

☐ The Islamic law of inheritance served as an drive behind the development of algebra (Arabic: al-jabr) by Muhammad ibn Mūsā al-Khwārizmī and other medieval Islamic mathematicians. Al-Khwārizmī's Hisab al-jabr w'al-muqabala had a chapter formulating the rules of inheritance as linear equations (& his knowledge of quadratic equations was unnecessary). Later mathematicians dedicated to the Islamic law of inheritance included Al-Hassār, who developed the modern symbol for fractions in the 12th century, and Abū al-Hasan ibn Alī al-Qalasādī, who developed an algebraic notation which affected the rise towards the introduction of algebraic symbols in the 15th century.

Figure 10 mathematics present in Quran

sent them to Bi'r-'Maune to convey the Islamic message; but they were ambushed & trapped making them all martyrs. More importantly, this knowledge enables man to understand his purpose which when attained brings new meaning and structure to his/her life...This further removes stress, and often other burdensome ideas of daily life that plague people who have become disconnected. This connection is in fact the connection that enables the highest states of being, and due to this warm and sincere interest which was encouraging to youth, young Companions matured to the point of sacrificing their lives, property, and families on Allah's path...

Jafir ibn Abi Talib (d. A H.)

Jafir was the son of the Prophet's uncle, Abu Talib, and Ali's older brother. These words spoken by Jafir Ibn Abi Talib (ra) to Najashee when he immigrated to Abyssinia as a result of persecution from the Meccans, show his knowledge and self-confidence as a youth:

"O King! We were an ignorant society that worshipped idols, ate dead meat, made every kind of prostitution, cut off ties with our relatives, and treated our neighbors badly. The strong among us oppressed the weak. We were like this until Allah sent us a Messenger from among us whose genealogy, truthfulness, trustworthiness and chastity we know. The Prophet sent to us called us to believe in the unity of God {he is ONE}, to serve Him, and to abandon the rocks and idols our fathers worshipped. He called us to be truthful, to fulfill trusts, to continue relations with relatives, to be a good neighbor, to desist from what is haram {forbidden} and from spilling blood {without legal right}, and he forbid us to make prostitution, lying as a witness, violating the property of orphans, and slandering respectable women... He only commanded us to serve Allah and not to take partners with Him, and to pray, give alms and fast." "We immediately affirmed him {Muhammad s.a.w}, believed in him and **conformed to what he brought from God**. We only served Allah and we did not attribute any partners to Him. We accepted as haram {forbidden} what He made haram and halal {permissible} what He made halal.."

Usama Ibn Zayd (d. 54 H.)

Usama is the son of Zayd Ibn Harithah, the Prophet's foster child and freed slave. He was "Habibu Rasulullah" or a youth loved and befriended by the Prophet. Shortly before the death of the Prophet, Usama was appointed as commander of the Sahaba (ra) army that was to be sent to Mu'tah in which were found Abu Bakr (ra) and Umar (ra). Due to this appointment, some began to indicate their criticism, anxiety and displeasure. Hearing their criticisms, the Prophet ordered a sermon to be prepared to the effect that some people had criticized Usama's appointment; Undoubtedly, while appointing Usama, a non-Arab youth, as commander of hundreds of prominent Sahaba (ra), he wanted to show actively that in Islam's preferred understanding of command it was not class and age that were essential, but capability and worthiness. Of course, there were more experienced older Companions in Usama's army. However, the Prophet's appointing a freedman as commander was very important in respect to implanting in their minds that in commandership, class and tribal factors have no importance and in respect to providing opportunities to youth regardless of which social segment they are from. Those with their natural characteristics who had not yet escaped from the effects of the Age of Ignorance culture and bigotry and who had not yet fully adopted Islamic teaching; On the other hand, many Sahaba, including Abu Bakr (ra) who asked permission from Usama (ra) for Umar (ra) who needed to stay in Medina, obeyed Usama (ra) both in regard to the Prophet's appointment and after his death in regard to approval from the Caliph and sending Usama (ra) to battle. Thus, they proved once again how meritorious they and Islam were.

Mus'ab Ibn Umayr Ibn Hashim (d. 3 H.)

A member of Mecca's wealthiest and noblest family {Banū ʿAbd al-Dār branch of the Quraysh tribe.}; Mus'ab was raised in comfort and abundance. He was liked by everyone for his way of dressing, his courtesy and his physique. He was an extremely intelligent youth and, due to his fine and clear speech, everyone envied him. There was no worldly blessing Mus'ab had not attained. However, he was in a spiritual crisis. Eventually he went to the Prophet who was in Arkam's house and became Muslim. Mus'ab ibn Umair was appointed the first ambassador of Islam and was sent to Yathrib (Medina) to prepare the city for the forthcoming Hijra of the prophet s.a.w. and the Muslims who didn't migrate to Abyssinia with the likes of Jafir (ra).

Arqam b. Abi'l-Arqam (d. 55)

One of the first converts to Islam, Arkam's house next to the Safa Peak became a headquarters for the Prophet and other Muslims. Tied with loyalty to the Prophet, he put his house under the Prophet's command. Finding this house, called the "Daru'l-Arqam" in Islamic history, to be very suitable for Islamic activities, the Prophet made it into a center. At first, the Prophet s.a.w would call people to Islam in this house, and he would teach them how to worship here. Muslims also hid in this house to escape the persecution of the idolaters of Mecca; Opening his house, which was just next to the Kaaba, for the call to Islam when he was only a youth of 17-18, shows what a very brave and self-sacrificing young man he was.

Mu'adh Ibn Jabal (d. 18 H)

When the prophet s.a.w sent Mu'adh (ra) to Yemen to teach the people about Islam, he personally bade farewell to him and walked for some distance alongside Mu'adh as he set out to leave the city. He was only 27 yrs. Old when he was sent. It is said that Mu'adh Ibn Jabal (ra) advised his son, "My son! Pray the prayer of he who is just about to leave and imagine that you might not be able to pray ever again. Know that the believer dies between two good deeds; one that he performed and one that he intended to perform later on."

Asma bint Abu Bakr (d. 73 H.)

One of the first Muslim young women was Aisha's (ra) older sister Asma (ra). Her name first became prominent at the time the Prophet s.a.w was making preparations for their leaving Mecca. Carrying food at night to the cave where the Prophet (s.a.w) and Abu Bakr (r.a) hid for three days during the Hijrah to Medina, Asma (ra) divided her waistband in two and tied the bag of provisions with one. The Prophet (saw) complimented her saying, "May Allah give you two waistbands in heaven for this one," and she is known as "Hizam'an" (two waistbands) as a result of this. During those days a group including Abu Jahil came and asked where Asma's (ra) father was. When she said, "I don't know," Abu Jahil struck her...

Aisha bint Abu Bakr (ra) (d. 58 H.)

Aisha (ra) learned religious sciences from the Prophet himself. Because she shared the same house with Islam's teacher and because it was next to the

Masjid, she benefited from his teachings night and day. Listening to his teachings and conversations, she immediately asked and learned anything she did not understand or was curious about or did not know. Due to the spiritual enlightenment that she got from the Prophet, Aisha became the most distinguished teacher of Islamic principles. Not only reporting the Sunnah and commenting on it, at the same time she put forth the mentality of scholastic criticism on the matter of its being understood correctly. Due to her strong memory, she gave unequalled service in the transmission of hadith and Sunnah to later generations. With the 2210 hadiths she reported that other Sahaba (ra) were without; they were more conclusive to the intimate setting of private life something she benefited from tremendously. Something I find interesting, that Allah would preserve this for A'isha (ra) a woman who is best at conveying those intimacies and details with emotional fullness to complete its understanding... Both men and women, would frequently visit her to consult with her and, to get her knowledge on their issues, to listen to her guidance and suggestions, and even to resolve their marital problems and to request her supplication. Her door was even open to enemies who stood against her in former years. Her house was like a center for knowledge, wisdom, guidance and consultation, and it was full of people every day...

Tasks, some small some great are all note-worthy and consecrated in history, and highly regarded deeds to Allah in the hereafter. We ourselves and our children need not discount any deed and do our best in contributing to the long list of those who gave something for the sake of Allah...

Health Care

Health Care for a long time now has suffered from rising cost due largely to lawsuits for malpractice {medical mistakes} some of which aren't resultant to negligence, however it has caused health care cost to sky rocket. In turn, employers who have tried to protect or increase their bottom lines, seek to employ the more healthy fit, in order to keep doctors' visits to a minimum. The domino effect that derives from the hub of health care shoots out in all direction. Here are 10 prominent frustrations behind health care in America:

1) **We spend the most.** We spend more than any other country in the world. In 2005, our per capita -- so, per person -- spending was $6,697. The next highest in the study was Canada, at $3,326 which is half. And remember -- that's "mean" spending, so it's the amount we spend divided by our population. But unlike in Canada, about 16 percent of our population *doesn't have insurance*, and so often can't use the system. These facts should set the stage for all numbers that come after: Every time you see a data point in which we're dead last, or not leading the pack, remember that we spend *twice* as much as any of our competitors.

2) **We don't pay doctors according to the quality of their care.** One of the first questions is "percent of primary care practices with financial incentives for quality" -- in other words, how many doctors are paid, in part, according to the quality of the care they deliver. In the United Kingdom, the number is 95 percent. In Australia, it's 72 percent. The U.S. scores lower than anyone else, at 30 percent. Similarly, electronic medical records -- which both increase the quality of care and lower its cost -- have 89 percent penetration in the U.K., 79 percent in Australia, 98 percent in the Netherlands, and 28 percent in America. On both these metrics, we perform miserably.

3) **Our wait times are low because many of us aren't getting care at all.** It's true; Americans do have short waits for non-elective surgeries. Only 4 percent of us wait more than six months. That's more than in Germany and the Netherlands, but considerably less than the Canadians (14 percent) or the Britons (15 percent). But our high performance on the waiting times only account for individuals who *get* the care they need. Our advantage dissipates when you see the next question, which asks how many patients skip care due to cost. And here brings the whole picture into better view, since Americans are far worse than anywhere else. In just the past year, a full 25 percent of us didn't visit the doctor when sick because we couldn't afford it. Twenty-three percent skipped a test, treatment, or follow-up recommended by a doctor. Another 23 percent didn't fill a prescription. No other country is even close to this sort of income-based rationing. In Canada, only 4 percent skipped a doctor's visit, and only 5 percent skipped care. In the U.K., those numbers are 2 percent and 3 percent. Few of our countrymen are waiting

for the care they need, that much is true. But that doesn't mean they're getting it quickly. Rather, about a quarter of us *aren't getting it at all*.

4) **Most of us don't have a regular physician.** One might expect, given what we pay, that our care would at least be more central and convenient. But it's not so. Of everyone surveyed, Americans were the least likely to report a doctor or general practitioner they routinely saw. As a result, Americans are the most likely to say their doctor doesn't know important information about their medical history, which has obvious implications for care quality, medical errors, etc.

5) **Care isn't particularly convenient.** Nor is medical service more convenient for Americans to access. On such question is whether your doctor has early morning hours, evening availability, or weekend slots... a full 67 percent of Americans -- more than in any other country -- say it's difficult to get care on nights, weekends, or holidays with resorting to the emergency room, where care is costlier and, if your injury is not grievous, less efficient.

6) **Our doctors don't listen to us.** But maybe the amount we're paying comes in customer service by which the medical staff is usually only seen—while the doctors spend only what is necessary time with us, before shifting to the next room focusing on the quantity of patients seen in order to make them all billable. No more reassuring, or more attentive to our cases; and vice-versa in terms of getting concise information that is well understood.

7) **We have high rates of chronic conditions.** Americans have the highest rate of chronic disease. And this isn't only a comparative problem; our high rates of chronic disease are a massive cost-driver for about 2/3rds the rise in health spending over the past few decades.

8) **But we're not treating them properly.** So given the high prevalence of such diseases, and the pressures they exert on our system, you'd expect the population to be more pro-active toward the illegal, political deviations misappropriating water sources or agriculture for example, and public relations advertisement & encouragement of illicit foods and products that in fact induce these diseases.

9) **We're frequent victims of medical, medication, and lab errors.** Along with Australians, Americans are the most likely to report a medical, medication, or lab error, with 20 percent saying they've experienced one of the above over the past year. For those of us with chronic diseases, the rates are even higher. There are many reasons for this, ranging from our low adoption rate of electronic medical records to our splintered care system. But the effects are bad for our health and, needless to say, bad for our insurance rates. Conservatives make a huge deal out of medical malpractice claims, but studies show that our high rate of lawsuits is due to our high rate of medical error. The crisis isn't just in the courtrooms; it's on the operating tables.

10) **Most of us are dissatisfied with our current system.** In health polling, happiness with the system is generally measured through a three-answer question:

   a. Does your system merely need minor changes, as it works pretty well?
   b. Does it need fundamental changes?
   c. Or does it need to be rebuilt?

   Of all the countries surveyed -- including the supposedly dystopic U.K. and Canada -- Americans are the least likely to report relative satisfaction, and the most likely to call for a fundamental rebuilding. Only 16 percent of us are happy. In Canada and the U.K., that number is 26 percent. In the Netherlands, it's 42 percent. Meanwhile, 34 percent of Americas want to completely rebuild... Only 12 percent of Canadians say the same, and only 15 percent of U.K. residents want a new system. So paying more than twice as much as anyone else, we have *the lowest* satisfaction with our health care system.

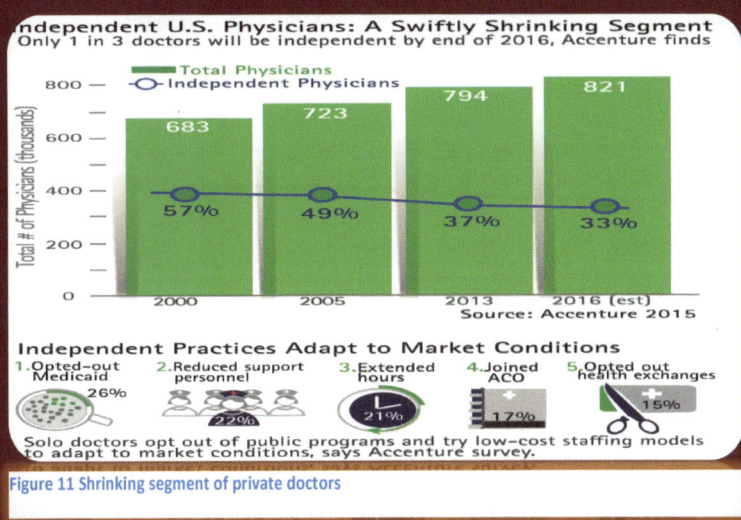

Independent U.S. Physicians: A Swiftly Shrinking Segment
Only 1 in 3 doctors will be independent by end of 2016, Accenture finds

Independent Practices Adapt to Market Conditions

1. Opted-out Medicaid — 26%
2. Reduced support personnel — 22%
3. Extended hours — 21%
4. Joined ACO — 17%
5. Opted out health exchanges — 15%

Solo doctors opt out of public programs and try low-cost staffing models to adapt to market conditions, says Accenture survey.

Figure 11 Shrinking segment of private doctors

Medicine is a profession, but health care itself is a business... A business that doesn't see profits in cures, but instead in the revolving door of treatment. This turning of medicine into business has resulted in the shift of doctors returning back to hospitals from private practice. Studies show that one-in-three will remain in independent practice according to a report by Accenture (Accenture , 2015). In Qur'an, Allah (subhana wa ta'ala) reminds us that if we are grateful for what he gives us, then He will increase our blessings. On the other hand, if we are ungrateful, and act as if Allah owes us something, His favours and blessing will be taken away and we will suffer a severe punishment: Another way of understanding is when we obey Allah's prohibitions we experience health and if we choose otherwise in indulging in those things prohibited then we experience disease...

Total Number of All U.S. <u>Registered</u> * Hospitals	5,627
Number of U.S. **<u>Community</u>** ** Hospitals	4,926
Number of Nongovernment Not-for-Profit Community Hospitals	2,870
Number of Investor-Owned (For-Profit) Community Hospitals	1,053
Number of State and Local Government Community Hospitals	1,003

Number of Federal Government Hospitals	213
Number of Non-federal Psychiatric Hospitals	403
Number of Non-federal Long Term Care Hospitals	75
Number of Hospital Units of Institutions (Prison Hospitals, College Infirmaries, Etc.)	10
Total Staffed Beds in All U.S. <u>Registered</u> * Hospitals	902,202
Staffed Beds in Community** Hospitals	786,874
Total Admissions in All U.S. <u>Registered</u> * Hospitals	34,878,887
Admissions in Community** Hospitals	33,066,720
Total Expenses for All U.S. <u>Registered</u> * Hospitals	$892,701,370,000
Expenses for Community** Hospitals	$808,869,209,000
Number of Rural Community** Hospitals	1,855
Number of Urban Community** Hospitals	3,071
Number of Community Hospitals in a <u>System</u> ***	3,183
Number of Community Hospitals in a <u>Network</u> ****	1,619

*Registered hospitals are those hospitals that meet AHA's criteria for registration as a hospital facility

**Community hospitals are defined as all non-federal, short-term general, and other special hospitals

1) Other special hospitals include obstetrics and gynecology; eye, ear, nose, and throat; rehabilitation; orthopedic; and other individually described specialty services.

   Community hospitals include academic medical centers or other teaching hospitals if they are non-federal short-term hospitals.

2) Excluded are hospitals not accessible by the general public, such as prison hospitals or college infirmaries.

***System is defined by AHA as either a multihospital or a diversified single hospital system

- A multihospital system is two or more hospitals owned, leased, sponsored, or contract managed by a central organization
- Single, freestanding hospitals may be categorized as a system by bringing into membership three or more, and at least 25 percent, of their owned or leased non-hospital pre-acute or post-acute health care organizations
- System affiliation does not preclude network participation.

**** Network is a group of hospitals, physicians, other providers, insurers and/or community agencies that work together to coordinate and deliver a broad spectrum of services to their community.

Network participation does not preclude system affiliation. [AHA Hospital Statistics, 2016 edition]

Positive Psychology

*B*ecause It is well known that the brain is an electrochemical organ; researchers have speculated that a fully functioning brain can generate as much as 10 watts of electrical power. From the 10 billion or so interconnected nerves cells if discharged all at once would produce five-millionths to 50 millionths of a volt.

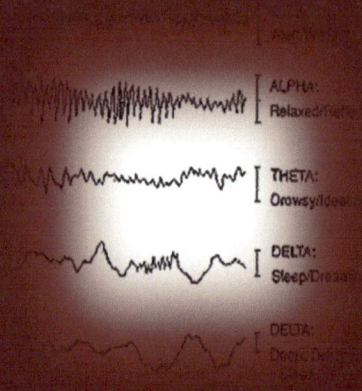

Figure 12 4 types of brain wave patterns

The reason for variance depends on the amount of active brain arousal. Beta waves are low in amplitude and are the fastest of the four different brain waves with a 15 to 40 hertz cycle. These waves occur during mental arousal. Again the variance in frequency like that of voltage depends on the stimulus of arousal. Having a normal conversation is enough for beta waves to occur, but someone engaged in debated would be on the higher end of the frequency range. Alpha brain waves are opposite to beta and represent the brain in non-arousal status. Slower & higher in amplitude with 9 to 14 hertz frequency, sitting down to relax, or meditation is an action that often induces alpha wave states. Theta waves have 5 to 8 hertz frequency, even slower with higher amplitude and are common in day dreaming. However, this condition doesn't suggest a resting state of the body; instead it's a mental relaxation that occurs. Freeway, driving, brushing the teeth, or even while running anything that cause the person to go onto auto pilot which is usually a very positive state. The last state delta is the slowest and highest in amplitude of them all with a frequency range of 1.5 to 4 hertz. This range never goes down to zero because that would indicate brain death. Among its complexities our brains have proven to maintain all four wave patterns in trace amounts at minimum even while having a dominant wave of activity or inactivity.

Deep, dreamless sleep would take a person down to this range. When delta waves increase into the frequency of theta waves this is when dreaming occurs. This can be witnessed with something called REM (rapid eye movement) where the eyes moved underneath the eyelid; Humans dream in 90 minute cycles that coincide with sleep cycles to different stages of brain wave activity. (Herrmann, 1997)

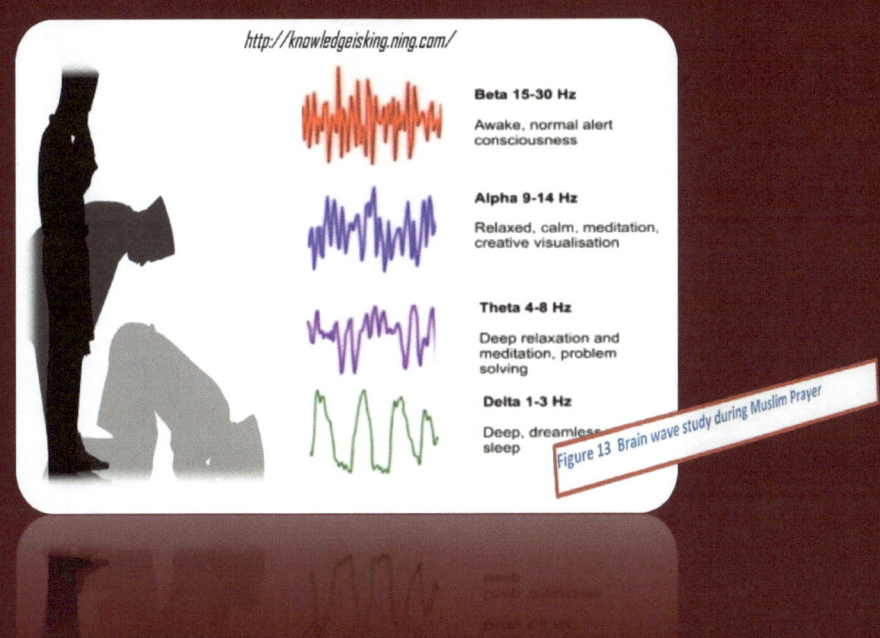

Figure 13 Brain wave study during Muslim Prayer

Seeking more scientific conclusion to the status of ourselves, other experiments have been undertaken to understanding the significance physically to our spiritual guidance and rejuvenation through the prayer... One such researcher is Andrew Newberg, one of Americas leading neuroscientist at the University of Pennsylvania Medical School. His research was taking (SPECT) single photon emission computed tomography scans of the brain while inactive in meditation vs meditative/prayer states.

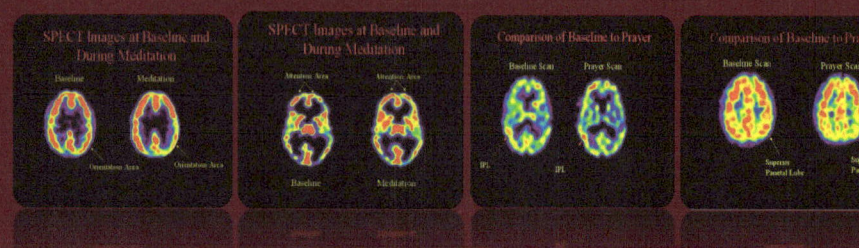

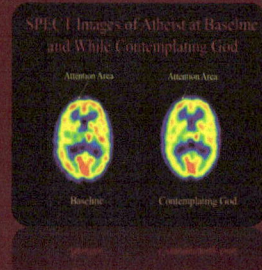

(Newberg). *From left to right scan 1 to 5*

By measuring the blood flow the certain areas of the brain, the scans record the various colors of red, yellow, green, blue & black. These colors represent the intensity of blood flow with red being the most active.

1. Buddhist monks exhibited decreased activity in the parietal lobes shows in yellow (2nd scan from left bottom right corner of right image) which meditation decreases our sense of space & time which is controlled in this area.

2. The front part of the brain that controls attention & concentration was seen to be more active during meditation represented in red. This coincides with the required amount of concentration needed for successful meditation.

3. Is the scan of the Nuns in prayer which indicated increased activity in the inferior parietal lobe (language area). This coincided with their verbal method of prayer unlike the more visual practice of the monks.

4. Both the nuns and monks experienced decreased activity in the orientation area of the superior parietal lobe. Mr. Newberg summarizes this from four basic components of belief: perception, emotions, cognition, and social interactions...Thinking over these four components we can see that it excludes the soul and it's strictly a premise based on

physical existence which carries understanding with it from that aspect alone. But, the human being is dual natured and exist of two components the physical body, and the soul in which the essence of life resides. The source of the spirit is from a divine source which we are connected; however once the spirit merges with the physical body it becomes susceptible to misguidance and corruption which takes it off course. During the years a child is unable to resist intellectually its environment it is not blameworthy, but the old adage phrase "the sins of the father visit the children" is giving a face for their responsibility to correctly guide the child on its natural course of Fitrah (human nature to worship one god). Hence the importance of personal search of truth, and purpose of life beyond the age of maturity which is the gift of individualism & choice not inheritance unless its correct...This gift, if used in unbiased ways, with sincerity of its search, can regain the course in which it entered the world by freeing itself from slavery of the lower self and its surroundings regaining its harmony. عنْ أَبِي هُرَيْرَةَ أَنَّهُ كَانَ يَقُولُ قال رَسُولُ الله صَلَّى الله عليه وسلّم ما من مَوْلُودٍ إلَّا يولَدُ على الْفِطْرَةِ فَأَبَواهُ يُهَوِّدانه ويُنَصِّرانه ويمَجِّسانه كما تُنْتَج النَّبِيمَةُ بَهيمةُ جمعاء هلْ تُحِسُّونَ فيها من جَدعاء ثُمَّ يَقُولُ أَبُو هُرَيْرَةَ وَاقْرَءوا اِن شِئْتُمْ فِطْرةَ اللهِ الَّتِي فطَرَ النَّاسَ عَلَيْها لا تَبْدِيل لِخَلْقِ اللهِ Abu Huraira reported: The Messenger of Allah, peace and blessings be upon him, said, "No one is born except upon natural instinct, then his parents turn him into a Jew or Christian or Magian. As an animal produces their young with perfect limbs, do you see anything defective?" Abu Huraira said, "Recite the verse if you wish: Direct your face toward the religion, inclining to truth, the nature of Allah upon which He has created the people. No change should there be in the creation of Allah. That is the correct religion, but most of the people do not know." [Sahih Bukhari 1292, Sahih Muslim 2658] The natural instinct of man as well as all creation is the acknowledgement of the creator & our submission to that. We enter this world in a condition of submission towards those in charge of us, and they are then entrusted with our development, which should never resist that natural disposition we are born on...

5. This 5th scan is interesting because it's the scan of an atheist who is a long-term meditator. The scan reviled at rest showed no significant increase in frontal lobe activity which was present in other meditations. Dr. Newberg suggest that this implies that the individual is not able to

activate the structures involved in those activates prayer/meditation upon something they don't believe in.

وَإِذَا تُتْلَىٰ عَلَيْهِمْ آيَاتُنَا بَيِّنَاتٍ قَالَ الَّذِينَ كَفَرُوا لِلَّذِينَ آمَنُوا أَيُّ الْفَرِيقَيْنِ خَيْرٌ مَقَامًا وَأَحْسَنُ نَدِيًّا

And when Our verses are recited to them as clear evidences, those who disbelieve say to those who believe, "Which of [our] two parties is best in position and best in association?" [Surah Maryam 19:73]

وَكَمْ أَهْلَكْنَا قَبْلَهُم مِّن قَرْنٍ هُمْ أَحْسَنُ أَثَاثًا وَرِئْيًا

And how many a generation have We destroyed before them who were better in possessions and [outward] appearance? [Maryam 19:74]

قُلْ مَن كَانَ فِي الضَّلَالَةِ فَلْيَمْدُدْ لَهُ الرَّحْمَٰنُ مَدًّا ۚ حَتَّىٰ إِذَا رَأَوْا مَا يُوعَدُونَ إِمَّا الْعَذَابَ وَإِمَّا السَّاعَةَ فَسَيَعْلَمُونَ مَنْ هُوَ شَرٌّ مَكَانًا وَأَضْعَفُ جُندًا

Say, "Whoever is in error - let the Most Merciful extend for him an extension [in wealth and time] until, when they see that which they were promised - either punishment [in this world] or the Hour [of resurrection] - they will come to know who is worst in position and weaker in soldiers." [Maryam 19:75]

وَيَزِيدُ اللَّهُ الَّذِينَ اهْتَدَوْا هُدًى ۗ وَالْبَاقِيَاتُ الصَّالِحَاتُ خَيْرٌ عِندَ رَبِّكَ ثَوَابًا وَخَيْرٌ مَّرَدًّا

And Allah increases those who were guided, in guidance, and the enduring good deeds are better to your Lord for reward and better for recourse. [Maryam 19:76]

Part of his concluding information was that the brain has two functions self-maintenance and self-transcendence. Ironically religion serves to provide us with the same two functions. Unfortunately, the research was concluded when the idea of bring a scanning a Muslims brain was presented to him during their prayer...These scans are of those of Christian Nouns, and Buddhist Monks during meditation. What I contemplate on most in what his projected finding might be are not the differences in faith, but instead the methods in which we differ in prayer or remembrance of the creator. For example in the SPECT scans by Dr. Newberg, both of his chosen subjects have methods of closing the eyes while in prayer and or meditation, where we Muslims do not close the eyes during prayer but instead focus them on the place of prostration throughout the prayer...If the brain carries out these two functions of maintenance &

transcendence leaving the eyes open serves to see ourselves in both functions bringing the physical to a place of higher spiritual being; where closing the eyes would block the image of self in its current place of time therefore transcedency wouldn't be effective in bringing the entire self to higher spiritual planes of being...Al-nafs mut'mainnah {volume 1 has deeper clarification on pg 43) is something that also brings this concept to clear fruition. This is the highest state of being for anyone in the physical world, which is the level of prophets and the desired level we should all strive to attain. Pairing this with the before mentioned conclusion as well as that of my own thoughts, for me it sheds light on why the eyes are left open & not closed during prayer. This may not seem significant, but in other research conducted there just maybe something to this difference which gives new premise to why we don't close the eyes.

Hazem Doufesh, MSC, Fatimah Ibrahim, PhD, Noor Azina Ismail, PhD, and Wan Azman Wan Ahmad, at the Department of Biomedical Engineering, Faculty of Engineering, University of Malaya, Kuala Lumpur, Malaysia. Carried out experimental scans of the brain on Muslims during salah (prayer), differing from Dr. Newberg's methods of SPECT scans, they incorporate the electronic/electrical scans of the brains wave patterns to gather evidence of the brains activity during prayer.

Methods: Thirty healthy Muslim men participated in the study. Their electrocardiograms and EEGs were continuously recorded before, during, and after *salat* practice with a computer-based data acquisition system (MP150, BIOPAC Systems Inc., Camino Goleta, California). Power spectral analysis was conducted to extract the RPα and HRV components. To avoid any artifacts due to physical movements, only four static positions (standing, bowing, sitting, and prostrating) were analyzed; the signals in between movements were excluded. Relative power spectra of the α band {which is alpha brain waves} frequency of EEG and ANS activities represented by the frequency bands of

HRV during *salat* measured using this equation. Where *fmax*=95 HZ, *fl*=8 HZ, *fh*=13 HZ. Fmax=frequency max; fl=frequency low; fh=frequency high

Results: During *salat*, a significant increase ($p<.05$) was observed in the mean RPα in the occipital and parietal regions and in the normalized unit of high-frequency (nuHF) power of HRV (as a parasympathetic index). (Altern, 2014)

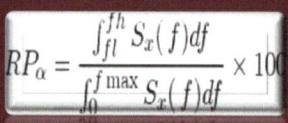

$$RP_\alpha = \frac{\int_{fl}^{fh} S_x(f)df}{\int_0^{f \max} S_x(f)df} \times 100$$

Figure 14 relative power alpha wave equation

Meanwhile, the normalized unit of low-frequency (nuLF) power and LF/HF of HRV (as sympathetic indices) decreased according to HRV analyses. RPα showed a significant positive correlation in the occipital and parietal electrodes with nuHF and significant negative correlations with nuLF and LF/HF. (Altern, 2014)

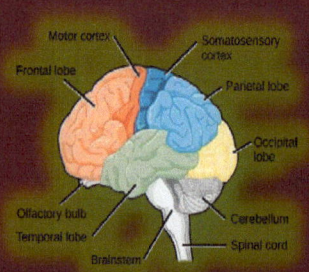

Figure 15 Brain Sections

The Occipital portion is primarily the visual area of the brain which receives input from the retina {via the thalamus} where different groups of neurons encode the varying difference in the information. The two important pathways originating from the occipital lobes are the dorsal and ventral streams. The dorsal projects to the parietal lobe & processes where the objects located; The Ventral stream projects to temporal lobes and processes where objects are. On the other hand the parietal lobe helps to put the world into perspective by integrating all of the sensory information from the ventral & dorsal pathways. This allows us to maneuver our environments, manipulate objects, as well as attentional awareness.

This unique liking of these two areas of the brain and there functions suggest that we have the ability to change our realities at will through this varying status of the conscious mind that peers into the subconscious which creates our reality. Deeper yet, the areas of the brain that help us in seeing our physical world are also active when we enter the spiritual world sight...Our reality is therefore not controlled by outside influences, but it is instead controlled and tempered by our mind states which consist of our thoughts &

beliefs. Contentment & tranquility would fall into this measure of spiritual exercise and the need or better yet designed designation of Muslims 5 times daily (excluding the super-regulatory prayers) we can then see the deliberate intent of Allah towards our achievement of higher altered realities through Salah. Body posturing during prayer is also something regarded that brings more focus, and increases alpha wave activity by reducing tension, and increased relaxation. What we do of what Allah has prescribed for us we see that those things provide benefit, but what we do from the things that have been made in-permissive there is disease...

All of this pre-information is suggestive toward the model of positive psychology which tends to focus on preventative measures rather than on treatment...Good for both the community and the individual, the science behind this idea is that each of us wants to lead a meaningful life, to cultivate what is best within ourselves to enhance our experiences in love, work & play. I find it necessary to mention this growing field in modern medicine especially after the long introduction on the mental states during prayer. For Muslims it should be understood, and far superior to the science of the modern world that still largely ignorance the dual nature of human-beings and is still searching for ways to appease the innate being through secular ways. Nonetheless, it's still worth mentioning because it sort of parallels the whole idea of Islam {submission to Allah} in serving both the inner & outer man/woman.

Positive psychology, with an initial appearance of the study in 2005, intends to intervene between the need of treatment by encouraging better thoughts, beliefs and behavior in preventing altogether the need of treatment by focusing on prevention. Things such as gratitude exercises which are designed to boost individual happiness & buffer people from the deleterious effects of depression. Other similar exercises are but not limited too are: Positive memory and positive self-information, which also are designed to cater to positive thoughts and a more positive outlook on one's self respectively. The ideals are great but realistically it not consider one simple principle about life...

Life is cylindrical...nothing is constant nor is it linear. Life represents more so the sinusoidal wave form this formation seems to also have relevant correlation to everything: health/sickness, happiness/sadness, love/hate, even our faith is challenge with high states and lower states...What makes things positive is the recognition of the existence of its mate negative, and through that realization of reciprocity we are better able to function with growth.

In a nutshell just from the nomenclature itself you can easily see Islam is already at the forefront of this secular concept.

For most people when the word psychology is even mentioned or worst yet mentioning any visits to the psychiatrist provokes thoughts of craziness or someone is crazy. This view is what secular views have stained the science with negative images and or thoughts that accompany its mention. On the other hand Islam in terms of psychology is actually the science of the spirit and its interaction with its physical existence. Our psychological conditions are therefore held intact through our link with the creator, which are enabled with the ability to grow and transcend worldly states of being which serve to rejuvenate, aspire, and give patience to us in whatever condition we may be. But, If we act otherwise then the doors of punishment {sicknesses, disease, loss of wealth, loss of faith, loss of calm, loss of stable mind states, happiness etc.} open upon us and our society in worldly life with more severe punishment awaiting us in the life to come. The felicity of what our real purpose of life is and its punishing characteristics are brought to life through the following story...

1. المص *Alif-Lam-Mim-Sad.* [These letters are one of the miracles of the Qur'an and none but Allah (Alone) knows their meanings].

٢. كِتَابٌ أُنزِلَ إِلَيْكَ فَلَا يَكُن فِي صَدْرِكَ حَرَجٌ مِّنْهُ لِتُنذِرَ بِهِ وَذِكْرَىٰ لِلْمُؤْمِنِينَ

[This is] a Book revealed to you, [O Muhammad] - so let there not be in your breast distress therefrom - that you may warn thereby and as a reminder to the believers. (This is the) Book (the Qur'an) sent down unto you (O Muhammadﷺ), so let not your breast be narrow therefrom, that you warn thereby, and a reminder unto the believers.

3. اتَّبِعُوا مَا أُنزِلَ إِلَيْكُم مِّن رَّبِّكُمْ وَلَا تَتَّبِعُوا مِن دُونِهِ أَوْلِيَاءَ ۗ قَلِيلًا مَّا تَذَكَّرُونَ [Say (O Muhammad ﷺ) to these idolaters (pagan Arabs) of your folk:] Follow what has been sent down unto you from your Lord (the Qur'an and Prophet Muhammad's *Sunnah*), and follow not any *Auliya'* (protectors and helpers, etc. who order you to associate partners in worship with Allah), besides Him (Allah). Little do you remember!

4. وَكَم مِّن قَرْيَةٍ أَهْلَكْنَاهَا فَجَاءَهَا بَأْسُنَا بَيَاتًا أَوْ هُمْ قَائِلُونَ And a great number of towns (their population) We destroyed (for their crimes). Our torment came upon them (suddenly) by night or while they were sleeping for their afternoon rest.

5. فَمَا كَانَ دَعْوَاهُمْ إِذْ جَاءَهُم بَأْسُنَا إِلَّا أَن قَالُوا إِنَّا كُنَّا ظَالِمِينَ No cry did they utter when Our Torment came upon them but this: "Verily, we were *Zalimun* (polytheists and wrong-doers, etc.)".

6. فَلَنَسْأَلَنَّ الَّذِينَ أُرْسِلَ إِلَيْهِمْ وَلَنَسْأَلَنَّ الْمُرْسَلِينَ Then surely, We shall question those (people) to whom it (the Book) was sent and verily, We shall question the Messengers {prophets give those revelations}.

7. فَلَنَقُصَّنَّ عَلَيْهِم بِعِلْمٍ ۖ وَمَا كُنَّا غَائِبِينَ Then surely, We shall narrate unto them (their whole story) with knowledge, and indeed We were not absent.

8. وَالْوَزْنُ يَوْمَئِذٍ الْحَقُّ ۚ فَمَن ثَقُلَتْ مَوَازِينُهُ فَأُولَٰئِكَ هُمُ الْمُفْلِحُونَ And the weighing on that day (Day of Resurrection) will be the true (weighing) **.** So as for those whose scale (of good deeds) will be heavy, they will be the successful (by entering Paradise).

9. وَمَنْ خَفَّتْ مَوَازِينُهُ فَأُولَٰئِكَ الَّذِينَ خَسِرُوا أَنفُسَهُم بِمَا كَانُوا بِآيَاتِنَا يَظْلِمُونَ And as for those whose scale will be light, they are those who will lose their ownselves (by entering Hell) because they denied and rejected Our *Ayat* (proofs, evidences, verses, lessons, signs, revelations, etc.).

10. وَلَقَدْ مَكَّنَّاكُمْ فِي الْأَرْضِ وَجَعَلْنَا لَكُمْ فِيهَا مَعَايِشَ ۗ قَلِيلًا مَّا تَشْكُرُونَ And surely, We gave you authority on the earth and appointed for you therein provisions (for your life). Little thanks do you give.

11. وَلَقَدْ خَلَقْنَاكُمْ ثُمَّ صَوَّرْنَاكُمْ ثُمَّ قُلْنَا لِلْمَلَائِكَةِ اسْجُدُوا لِآدَمَ فَسَجَدُوا إِلَّا إِبْلِيسَ لَمْ يَكُن مِّنَ السَّاجِدِينَ And surely, We created you (your father Adam) and then gave you shape (the noble shape of a human being), then We told the angels, "Prostrate to Adam", and they prostrated, except *Iblis* (Satan), he refused to be of those who prostrate.

12. قَالَ مَا مَنَعَكَ أَلَّا تَسْجُدَ إِذْ أَمَرْتُكَ ۖ قَالَ أَنَا خَيْرٌ مِّنْهُ خَلَقْتَنِي مِن نَّارٍ وَخَلَقْتَهُ مِن طِينٍ (Allah) said: "What prevented you (O *Iblis*) that you did not prostrate, when I commanded you?" *Iblis* said: "I am better than him (Adam), You created me from fire, and him You created from clay."

13. قَالَ فَاهْبِطْ مِنْهَا فَمَا يَكُونُ لَكَ أَن تَتَكَبَّرَ فِيهَا فَاخْرُجْ إِنَّكَ مِنَ الصَّاغِرِينَ (Allah) said: "(O *Iblis*) get down from this (Paradise), it is not for you to be arrogant here. Get out, for you are of those humiliated and disgraced."

14. قَالَ أَنظِرْنِي إِلَىٰ يَوْمِ يُبْعَثُونَ (Iblis) said: "Allow me respite till the Day they are raised up (i.e. the Day of Resurrection)."

15. قَالَ إِنَّكَ مِنَ الْمُنظَرِينَ (Allah) said: "You are of those allowed respite."

16. قَالَ فَبِمَا أَغْوَيْتَنِي لَأَقْعُدَنَّ لَهُمْ صِرَاطَكَ الْمُسْتَقِيمَ (Iblis) said: "Because You have sent me astray, surely I will sit in wait against them (human beings) on Your Straight Path.

17. ثُمَّ لَآتِيَنَّهُم مِّن بَيْنِ أَيْدِيهِمْ وَمِنْ خَلْفِهِمْ وَعَنْ أَيْمَانِهِمْ وَعَن شَمَائِلِهِمْ ۖ وَلَا تَجِدُ أَكْثَرَهُمْ شَاكِرِينَ Then I will come to them from before them and behind them, from their right and from their left, and You will not find most of them as thankful ones (i.e. they will not be dutiful to You)."

18. قَالَ اخْرُجْ مِنْهَا مَذْءُومًا مَّدْحُورًا ۖ لَّمَن تَبِعَكَ مِنْهُمْ لَأَمْلَأَنَّ جَهَنَّمَ مِنكُمْ أَجْمَعِينَ (Allah) said (to Iblis) "Get out from this (Paradise) disgraced and expelled. Whoever of them (mankind) will follow you, then surely I will fill Hell with you all."

19. وَيَا آدَمُ اسْكُنْ أَنتَ وَزَوْجُكَ الْجَنَّةَ فَكُلَا مِنْ حَيْثُ شِئْتُمَا وَلَا تَقْرَبَا هَٰذِهِ الشَّجَرَةَ فَتَكُونَا مِنَ الظَّالِمِينَ "And O Adam! Dwell you and your wife in Paradise, and eat thereof as you both wish, but approach not this tree otherwise you both will be of the Zalimun (unjust and wrong-doers)."

20. فَوَسْوَسَ لَهُمَا الشَّيْطَانُ لِيُبْدِيَ لَهُمَا مَا وُورِيَ عَنْهُمَا مِن سَوْآتِهِمَا وَقَالَ مَا نَهَاكُمَا رَبُّكُمَا عَنْ هَٰذِهِ الشَّجَرَةِ إِلَّا أَن تَكُونَا مَلَكَيْنِ أَوْ تَكُونَا مِنَ الْخَالِدِينَ Then Shaitan (Satan) whispered suggestions to them both in order to uncover that which was hidden from them of their private parts (before); he said: "Your Lord did not forbid you this tree save you should become angels or become of the immortals."

21. وَقَاسَمَهُمَا إِنِّي لَكُمَا لَمِنَ النَّاصِحِينَ And he [Shaitan (Satan)] swore by Allah to them both (saying): "Verily, I am one of the sincere well-wishers for you both."

22. فَدَلَّاهُمَا بِغُرُورٍ ۚ فَلَمَّا ذَاقَا الشَّجَرَةَ بَدَتْ لَهُمَا سَوْآتُهُمَا وَطَفِقَا يَخْصِفَانِ عَلَيْهِمَا مِن وَرَقِ الْجَنَّةِ ۖ وَنَادَاهُمَا رَبُّهُمَا أَلَمْ أَنْهَكُمَا عَن تِلْكُمَا الشَّجَرَةِ وَأَقُل لَّكُمَا إِنَّ الشَّيْطَانَ لَكُمَا عَدُوٌّ مُّبِينٌ So he misled them with deception. Then when they tasted of the tree, that which was hidden from them of their shame (private parts) became manifest to them and they began to stick together the leaves of Paradise over themselves (in order to cover their shame). And their Lord called out to them (saying): "Did I not forbid you that tree and tell you: Verily, Shaitan (Satan) is an open enemy unto you?"

23. قَالَا رَبَّنَا ظَلَمْنَا أَنفُسَنَا وَإِن لَّمْ تَغْفِرْ لَنَا وَتَرْحَمْنَا لَنَكُونَنَّ مِنَ الْخَاسِرِينَ They said: "Our Lord! We have wronged ourselves. If You forgive us not, and bestow not upon us Your Mercy, we shall certainly be of the losers."

24. قَالَ اهْبِطُوا بَعْضُكُمْ لِبَعْضٍ عَدُوٌّ ۖ وَلَكُمْ فِي الْأَرْضِ مُسْتَقَرٌّ وَمَتَاعٌ إِلَىٰ حِينٍ (Allah) said: "Get down, one of you an enemy to the other [i.e. Adam, Hawwa (Eve), and Shaitan (Satan), etc.]. On earth will be a dwelling-place for you and an enjoyment, - for a time."

25. قَالَ فِيهَا تَحْيَوْنَ وَفِيهَا تَمُوتُونَ وَمِنْهَا تُخْرَجُونَ He said: "Therein you shall live, and therein you shall die, and from it you shall be brought out (i.e.resurrected)."

26. يَا بَنِي آدَمَ قَدْ أَنزَلْنَا عَلَيْكُمْ لِبَاسًا يُوَارِي سَوْآتِكُمْ وَرِيشًا ۖ وَلِبَاسُ التَّقْوَىٰ ذَٰلِكَ خَيْرٌ ۚ ذَٰلِكَ مِنْ آيَاتِ اللَّهِ لَعَلَّهُمْ يَذَّكَّرُونَ O Children of Adam! We have bestowed raiment upon you to cover yourselves (screen your private parts, etc.) and as an adornment, and the raiment of righteousness, that is better. Such are among the *Ayat* (proofs, evidences, verses, lessons, signs, revelations, etc.) of Allah, that they may remember (i.e. leave falsehood and follow truth).

27. يَا بَنِي آدَمَ لَا يَفْتِنَنَّكُمُ الشَّيْطَانُ كَمَا أَخْرَجَ أَبَوَيْكُم مِّنَ الْجَنَّةِ يَنزِعُ عَنْهُمَا لِبَاسَهُمَا لِيُرِيَهُمَا سَوْآتِهِمَا ۗ إِنَّهُ يَرَاكُمْ هُوَ وَقَبِيلُهُ مِنْ حَيْثُ لَا تَرَوْنَهُمْ ۗ إِنَّا جَعَلْنَا الشَّيَاطِينَ أَوْلِيَاءَ لِلَّذِينَ لَا يُؤْمِنُونَ O Children of Adam! Let not *Shaitan* (Satan) deceive you, as he got your parents [Adam and Hawwa (Eve)] out of Paradise, stripping them of their raiments, to show them their private parts. Verily, he and *Qabiluhu* (his soldiers from the jinns or his tribe) see you from where you cannot see them. Verily, We made the *Shayatin* (devils) *Auliya'* (protectors and helpers) for those who believe not.

28. وَإِذَا فَعَلُوا فَاحِشَةً قَالُوا وَجَدْنَا عَلَيْهَا آبَاءَنَا وَاللَّهُ أَمَرَنَا بِهَا ۗ قُلْ إِنَّ اللَّهَ لَا يَأْمُرُ بِالْفَحْشَاءِ ۖ أَتَقُولُونَ عَلَى اللَّهِ مَا لَا تَعْلَمُونَ And when they commit a *Fahisha* (evil deed, going round the Ka'bah in naked state, every kind of unlawful sexual intercourse, etc.), they say: "We found our fathers doing it, and Allah has commanded us of it." Say: "Nay, Allah never commands of *Fahisha*. Do you say of Allah what you know not?

29. قُلْ أَمَرَ رَبِّي بِالْقِسْطِ ۖ وَأَقِيمُوا وُجُوهَكُمْ عِندَ كُلِّ مَسْجِدٍ وَادْعُوهُ مُخْلِصِينَ لَهُ الدِّينَ ۚ كَمَا بَدَأَكُمْ تَعُودُونَ Say (O Muhammad ﷺ): My Lord has commanded justice and (said) that you should face Him only (i.e. worship none but Allah and face the *Qiblah*, i.e. the Ka'bah at Makkah during prayers) in each and every place of worship, in prayers (and not to face other false deities and idols), and invoke Him only making your religion sincere to Him by not joining in worship any partner to Him and with the intention that you are doing your deeds for Allah's sake only. As He brought you (into being) in the beginning, so shall you be brought into being (on the Day of Resurrection) [in two groups, one as a blessed one (believers), and the other as a wretched one (disbelievers)].

Whenever Allah tells us of the wrongs, and of our potential failings he always gives us the antidote to our sickness that would return us back to a normal & better condition.

وَالْعَصْرِ

By the passage of time, [Al-Asr 103:1]

إِنَّ الْإِنْسَانَ لَفِي خُسْرٍ

Indeed, mankind is in loss,[Al-Asr 103:2]

إِلَّا الَّذِينَ آمَنُوا وَعَمِلُوا الصَّالِحَاتِ وَتَوَاصَوْا بِالْحَقِّ وَتَوَاصَوْا بِالصَّبْرِ

Except for those who have believed and done righteous deeds and advised each other to truth and advised each other to patience. [Al-Asr 103:3]

Surah al-Asr even in its brevity Allah speaks to the psychology of man...With the passage of time man gets more and more lost.

- Lost, because the truth about himself, his purpose, about his lord, and all the guidance of scripture through his chosen messengers/prophets has been lost or ignored with negative stigmas...
- Lost because religion is followed in inheritance not truth وَإِذَا قِيلَ لَهُمُ اتَّبِعُوا مَا أَنْزَلَ اللَّهُ قَالُوا بَلْ نَتَّبِعُ مَا أَلْفَيْنَا عَلَيْهِ آبَاءَنَا ۗ أَوَلَوْ كَانَ آبَاؤُهُمْ لَا يَعْقِلُونَ شَيْئًا وَلَا يَهْتَدُونَ

  And when it is said to them, "Follow what Allah has revealed," they say, "Rather, we will follow that which we found our fathers doing." Even though their fathers understood nothing, nor were they guided? [Al-Baqarah 2:170], Lost from the path of his own natural disposition, which makes life a constant struggle that is always opposing him, a struggle that can't be won in resistance and disunity...

EXCEPT {this is the Shart (Arabic for conditional word) that Allah use to answer the previous condition of mankind being lost}. Except:

- those who believe; belief is first because it precedes life... وَإِذْ أَخَذَ رَبُّكَ مِنْ بَنِي آدَمَ مِنْ ظُهُورِهِمْ ذُرِّيَّتَهُمْ وَأَشْهَدَهُمْ عَلَىٰ أَنْفُسِهِمْ أَلَسْتُ بِرَبِّكُمْ ۖ قَالُوا بَلَىٰ ۛ شَهِدْنَا ۚ أَنْ تَقُولُوا يَوْمَ الْقِيَامَةِ إِنَّا كُنَّا عَنْ هَٰذَا غَافِلِينَ

  And [mention] when your Lord took from the children of Adam - from their loins - their descendants and made them testify of themselves, [saying to them], "Am I not your Lord?" They said, "Yes, we have testified." [This] - Lest you should say on the day of Resurrection, "Indeed, we were of this unaware." [Al-A'raf 7:172]; life isn't life first without belief because through belief comes the solutions to why mankind is lost in the first place...Through belief our link to the creator, to each other, and to creation is re-established. Through belief the flood gates of blessings can be opened that would fill our lives and being in the world which the world itself would open in the fullness of what she has been created to give man.

- Through belief comes the acquisition of higher knowledge, through knowledge, our behaviors are modified through intention, and then everything we do becomes an act of worship {meaning it lies within the divine law}, and this would then propel man/woman to higher states of consciousness.

So how do we get there?   أَوْ تَقُولُوا إِنَّمَا أَشْرَكَ آبَاؤُنَا مِن قَبْلُ وَكُنَّا ذُرِّيَّةً مِّن بَعْدِهِمْ ۖ أَفَتُهْلِكُنَا بِمَا فَعَلَ الْمُبْطِلُونَ

Or [lest] you say, "It was only that our fathers associated [others in worship] with Allah before, and we were but descendants after them. {So the wrong doers will then ask} Then would you destroy us for what the falsifiers have done?" {In leading them astray; Falsifiers are those who people including parents, followed blindly without searching the truth} Allah answers simply by saying "advised each other to truth {which means ALL TRUTH} and advised each other to patience."{Knowing our true purpose we are then able to be patient, but patience cannot be without trust in Allah}. Forbidding what is evil and calling each other to what is good...counsel shouldn't just be thought of in terms of verbal communication nor should it only be regarded outside of ourselves. True counsel would begin with ourselves and extended into our communities through our own actions/behaviors. This is exactly why so many things don't manifest according to our one sided views. We often fail to see the reciprocity needed that would complete the verbal side of counsel. In other words we need to be that in which we call too or advise too. This is the psychology behind our mental states and the reason why things are so out of order psychologically for so many people. Public opinion has been swayed to non-belief {which includes wrong belief, association of partners to Allah, or just spoken words divorced from action that confirm what the mouth utters}. In addition, lewd acts of every kind are openly done in public, which further serve to negate our recipe for societal success. The recipe was given in 3 short ayat, which suggest its ease but humanity finds the easier things always the hardest to implement.

Coping

Since man has lost his way & purpose, he has lost sight of his true home so he has now occupied himself with the task of making his temporary home something of his on imagination of the eternal home. But no matter how hard he tries, no matter how much he accumulates or gathers the ills of the world still creep into his life plaguing him with the remembrance of his mortality & insignificance. Ignorant of the soul, so he focuses on medicine; ignorant of Jannah {heaven}, so he seeks it in this life; secular so his focus is greed; driven by desire, so his past time is consumption; shallow integrity so he depends on his wealth/title to win him followers; Held to his own rational thought, so he depends on his science...of which nothing sustains the felicity he tries to grasp. These mounting loses only add to his desperate aims that further mislead him into an abyss of chaos forever widening with darkness that envelopes his or her light that deadens the heart to a point in which it can no longer return...[Sayyar Isma'il Swift]

وَاتْلُ عَلَيْهِمْ نَبَأَ الَّذِي آتَيْنَاهُ آيَاتِنَا فَانسَلَخَ مِنْهَا فَأَتْبَعَهُ الشَّيْطَانُ فَكَانَ مِنَ الْغَاوِينَ

And recite to them, [O Muhammad], the news of him to whom we gave [knowledge of] Our signs, but he detached himself from them; so Satan pursued him, and he became of the deviators.[Al-A'raf 7:175]

وَلَوْ شِئْنَا لَرَفَعْنَاهُ بِهَا وَلَكِنَّهُ أَخْلَدَ إِلَى الْأَرْضِ وَاتَّبَعَ هَوَاهُ ۚ فَمَثَلُهُ كَمَثَلِ الْكَلْبِ إِن تَحْمِلْ عَلَيْهِ يَلْهَثْ أَوْ تَتْرُكْهُ يَلْهَث ۚ ذَّلِكَ مَثَلُ الْقَوْمِ الَّذِينَ كَذَّبُوا بِآيَاتِنَا ۚ فَاقْصُصِ الْقَصَصَ لَعَلَّهُمْ يَتَفَكَّرُونَ

And if We had willed, we could have elevated him thereby, but he adhered [instead] to the earth and followed his own desire. **So his example is like that of the dog: if you chase him, he pants, or if you leave him, he [still] pants. {No matter what the dog does to appease himself it doesn't seem to be fulfilling}** That is the example of the people who denied Our signs. So relate the stories that perhaps they will give thought. [Al-A'raf 7:176]

سَاءَ مَثَلًا الْقَوْمُ الَّذِينَ كَذَّبُوا بِآيَاتِنَا وَأَنفُسَهُمْ كَانُوا يَظْلِمُونَ

How evil an example [is that of] the people who denied Our signs and used to wrong themselves.[Al-A'raf 7:177]

مَن يَهْدِ اللَّهُ فَهُوَ الْمُهْتَدِي ۖ وَمَن يُضْلِلْ فَأُولَٰئِكَ هُمُ الْخَاسِرُونَ

Whoever Allah guides {Faith is a gift of those who seek their lord in truth} - he is the [rightly] guided; and whoever He sends astray {those who take religion as a joke, blind follow, and play} - it is those who are the losers.[Al-A'raf 7:178]

This life is designed by Allah to be an experience of test and trials, and through these test and trials we are meant to grow and get better...But when humanity fails to understand this is all part of the divine plan for us we fail ourselves.

وَمَا جَعَلْنَا لِبَشَرٍ مِّن قَبْلِكَ الْخُلْدَ ۖ أَفَإِن مِّتَّ فَهُمُ الْخَالِدُونَ

And We did not grant to any man before you eternity [on earth]; so if you die - would they be eternal? [Al-Anbiya 21:34]

كُلُّ نَفْسٍ ذَائِقَةُ الْمَوْتِ ۗ وَنَبْلُوكُم بِالشَّرِّ وَالْخَيْرِ فِتْنَةً ۖ وَإِلَيْنَا تُرْجَعُونَ

Every soul will taste death. And We test you with evil and with good as trial; and to Us you will be returned. [Al-Anbiya 21:35]

أَحَسِبَ النَّاسُ أَن يُتْرَكُوا أَن يَقُولُوا آمَنَّا وَهُمْ لَا يُفْتَنُونَ

Do the people think that they will be left to say, "We believe" and they will not be tried? [Al-Ankabut 29:2]

Then he tells us why we are tried: وَلَقَدْ فَتَنَّا الَّذِينَ مِن قَبْلِهِمْ ۖ فَلَيَعْلَمَنَّ اللَّهُ الَّذِينَ صَدَقُوا وَلَيَعْلَمَنَّ الْكَاذِبِينَ

But We have certainly tried those before them, and Allah will surely make evident those who are truthful, and He will surely make evident the liars.[Al-Ankabut 29:3]

The eternal home of Jannah {heaven} is pure and only the souls that achieve purity are allowed to dwell therein...That means the purification process of ourselves is undertaken through test and trials all necessary to better us and they are from among the mercies of our Lord that he has bestowed upon us in this worldly life as a means of helping us and making us more so worthy into dwell in his eternal abode...Like anything else worth attaining through hard work, the bettering of ourselves is the price we pay, but it's a price that we benefit from. This revenue used to purchase that eternal dwelling is an investment we make for ourselves.

These trials are not meant to oppress, but instead are there to help us grow. The human being without constant discipline falls into decadence...it's only by mental/physical/ spiritual parameters is he able to exceed previous statuses of his/herself. This is something that distinguishes those who submit verses those who refuse. Of those who refuse live much more difficult lives. Maybe on the outside the facades image they try to portray to the world is shallow with a lack of love and trust deep within their inner circles...overwhelming stresses that require medications to sleep, or intoxicants to cope with daily pressures... Trials when understood properly alleviate one from worry and enlighten him/her to the mercies of the Creator in trying them... "As recorded in Bukhari and Muslim"; The Prophet (sallallaahu 'alayhi wa sallam) said, "Whoever Allah wants good for him, he puts them to test. He puts them through difficulties. Like a diamond or some metal that has to be burnt and then that which is bad from it is removed so that you have that which is the pure diamond or the pure gold or whatever. Put them to tests, trials and difficulties."

Reason for this is to:
- purify us from sins and wrongs that we have done
- assist us in the true realization of reality
- Provide spiritual growth

Spiritual growth should be a normal consequence to trials we bear.

[Al-Ankabut 29:6]

ومن جاهد فإنّما يُجاهد لنفسه ۚ إنَّ الله لغنيٌّ عن العالمين

And whoever strives only strives for [the benefit of] himself. Indeed, Allah is free from need of the worlds. [Al-Ankabut 29:7]

والّذين آمنوا وعملوا الصّالحات لنُكفّرنّ عنهُم سيّئاتهم ولنَجزينّهُم أحسن الّذي كانُوا يعملُون

And those who believe and do righteous deeds - We will surely remove from them their misdeeds and will surely reward them according to the best of what they used to do.
Research proves that trauma helps people to embrace their faith more so than the absence of trauma. [Al-Hadid 57:22

مَا أَصَابَ مِن مُّصِيبَةٍ فِي الْأَرْضِ وَلَا فِي أَنفُسِكُمْ إِلَّا فِي كِتَابٍ مِّن قَبْلِ أَن نَّبْرَأَهَا ۚ إِنَّ ذَٰلِكَ عَلَى اللَّهِ يَسِيرٌ

No disaster strikes upon the earth or among yourselves except that it is in a register before We bring it into being - indeed that, for Allah, is easy [Al-Hadid 57:23

لِّكَيْلَا تَأْسَوْا عَلَىٰ مَا فَاتَكُمْ وَلَا تَفْرَحُوا بِمَا آتَاكُمْ ۗ وَاللَّهُ لَا يُحِبُّ كُلَّ مُخْتَالٍ فَخُورٍ

In order that you not despair over what has eluded you and not exult [in pride] over what He has given you. And Allah does not like everyone self-deluded and boastful - -

So, it becomes apparent that everything from the best of things to the worst of things is well within the encompassing knowledge and will of the Creator. Although things often escape the limitations of man's rational especially those who refuse to submit, we you might find within their lives more calamitous things occur only on account to bring them back to the lord. For some people it's the only time they remember Allah, so on that condition Allah keeps them in a perpetual state of tragedy for a time...only lighting the trauma briefly before introducing yet another challenging ordeal. This brings me to the question I hear many non-believers say about eternal punishment. Using their human logic they come to the conclusion of why will Allah punish someone for enter it's for things they did wrong in a shorter lifetime in comparison to eternity? The answer is quite simple when you contemplate the reasons of calamities...had he/she been give eternal life in the world they would have gone on acting and behaving in the wrong way therefore Allah is just in punishing them because he knows the hearts of his creation.

Times of crisis again are meant to redirect humanity back to submission {his natural disposition} toward recognition of his true self and divine framework the surrounds him/her. Uncovering false beliefs, principles, ideals and behaviors that otherwise turn him against his/her own harmonic state. One thing is for sure is we are way to insignificant to challenge our existence with the Creator much less believe as many people believe in negation of their responsibilities of pending accountability. It is in fact this Jihad with the self that poses to be the more formidable adversary.

Religion is therefore the guide to resilience in our ability to bounce back, persevere, and modify pre-existing thought, beliefs, behaviors that bring forth a stronger you...Allah swt is ALL GOOD and even when things appear evil, or bad there is good within it. This of course doesn't exclude the consequences of humanities on hand in mischief [Ash-Shura 42:30

وما أصابكُم مّن مُصيبةٍ فبما كسبَت أيديكُم ويعفُو عن كثيرٍ

And whatever strikes you of disaster - it is for what your hands have earned; but He {Allah} pardons much.

Holy Quran 29:38

وعادًا وثمُود وقد تَبَيّن لكُم مّن مّساكنِهِمْ ۖ وزيّن لهُم الشّيْطانُ أعمالهُم فصدّهُم عن السّبيل وكانُوا مُستبصرينَ

And [We destroyed] 'Aad and Thamud {two ancient nations in Arabia}, and it has become clear to you from their [ruined] dwellings {their corruption & wrongdoing}. And Satan had made pleasing to them their deeds and averted them from the path, and they were endowed with perception {which was overlooked due to their arrogance so}.
Humanity is no different from his ancestors, and now like then humanity is daring of a severe punishment that is very subtly coming into full view.

The secular world with all of its failing man-made systems is collapsing under its on weight of deception and trickery that has created for mankind a very different rendering of a world that is shared by all its inhabitants. It is therefore up to humanity to reformat its societal norms by attacking the sources of injustice & decomposition of the public psyche. These chaotic conditions are meant to further confuse the path that leads to truth while at the same time keep you and I from contentment by infusing artificial mind states upon the people of control and. coping with life is a natural ability and something we are designed to undertake.

Once there were three men from the children of Israel, a leper, a blind man and a bald man; whom Allah wanted to test, so He sent an angel to them. The angel asked the leper, 'What would you most like to have?' the leper said, 'Good complexion and good skin, because the people consider me to be filthy.' Then the angel touched him and he was cured. He was given a good complexion and good skin. Then the angel said, 'Which property would you most like to have?' The leper said, 'Camels.' So he was given a pregnant camel, and the angel said, 'May Allah bless you with it.'

Then the angel came to the bald man and said, 'What would you most like to have?' He said, "nice hair, and I wish to be cured from this disease because people find me repulsive.' The angel touched him, and he was given nice hair.' Then the angel said, 'Which property would you most like to have/' He said, 'Cows.' So the angel gave him a pregnant cow that had plenty of milk. The angel said to him, 'May Allah bless you with it.'

The angel came to the blind man and said, 'What would you most like to have?' He said, 'I wish Allah would restore my sight so I can see the people.' He touched his eyes and Allah gave him his sight back. The angel said, 'Which property would you most like to have?' He said, 'Sheep.' So the angel gave him a pregnant sheep. The angel said to him, 'May Allah bless you with it.'

Later, all three pregnant animals gave birth to their young. They multiplied and brought forth so many (animals) that one of the men had a herd of camels filling a valley, one had a herd of cows fillings a valley, and the other one had a flock of sheep filling a valley.

Then the angel, disguised to appear as a leper, visited the leper and said, 'I am a poor man, who has lost all means of livelihood while on a journey; so none will satisfy my need except Allah and then you. In the Name of Him who has given you such nice complexion, such beautiful skin, and so much property, I ask you to give me a camel so that I may reach my destination.'

The man replied, 'I have many obligations (so I cannot give any to you).' The angel said, 'I think I know you, were you not a leper who the people shunned? Weren't you a poor man and then Allah gave this to you?' He replied, 'I inherited this from my family.' The angel said, 'If you are lying, then let Allah make you as you were before.'

Then the angel, disguised as a bald man, went to the bald man and said the same as he had the leper. He too answered the same way. The angel told him, 'If you are lying, then let Allah make you as you were before.'

Then the angel, disguised as a blind man, visited the blind man and said, 'I am a poor man and I'm a traveller, whose means of livelihood have been exhausted while on a journey. I have nobody to help me except Allah, and after Him, you yourself. I ask you in the name of Him who has given you back your eyesight to give me a sheep, so that with its help, I may complete my journey.' The man said, 'I was once blind, and Allah returned my sight to me, I was once poor and Allah made me rich. So take anything you like from what I have. By Allah, I will not praise you for leaving anything (you need) of my property which you may take for Allah's sake.' The angel replied, 'Keep your property. You (three men) have been tested. Allah is pleased with you, but He is angry with your two companions...

Bibliography

Aamodt, S. (2012, October 15). *Are We Cooperative or Competitiv?* . Retrieved from Being Human : beinghuman.org

Accenture . (2015, July 29). *Many U.S. Doctors will leave private practice for hospital employment.* Retrieved from Accentue : https://newsroom.accenture.com/news/many-us-doctors-will-leave-private-practice-for-hospital-employment-accenture-reports.htm

Altern, J. (2014). Effect of Muslim Prayer (salat) on a Electroencephalography and its relationship with Autonomic Nervous System Activity. *Alternative and Complimetary Medicine* .

American Psychiatric Association. (2013). DSM-5 . In *Diagnostic and Statistical Manual of Mental Disorders* (p. 970). Washington D.C./ London : American Psychiatic Publishing .

Association of Gay & Lesbian Psychiatrist . (2011). *The History of Psychiatry & Homosexuality* . Retrieved from LGBT Mental Health Syllabus: http://www.aglp.org/gap/1_history/

Bale, L. S. (1992). *Gregory Bateson's Theory of Mind Pratical Applications to Pedagogy.* San Fransico : Chandler Publishing Company .

Bouhdiba, A. (1975). *Sexuality in Islam volume 20.* London & New York : Routledge Taylor & Francis Group .

Bunyamin Erul, P. (2010, March 5). *Young Sahaba in the Prophet's circle*. Retrieved from The Last
    Prophet : http://www.lastprophet.info/young-sahaba-in-the-prophet-s-circle

Carla Sharp, P. F. (2015). Borderline personality disorder in adolescence-recent conceptualization,
    intervention, and implications for clinical practice. *Prationer Review*.

Fay, M. (2016, January 7). *Overseas contingency operations spending and FY 2017 Budget request*.
    Retrieved from Niskanen Center : https://niskanencenter.org/blog/overseas-contingency-
    operations-spending-and-the-fy-2017-budget-request/

Herman, J. (2011, May 28). *Can Transgender people bear Children?* Retrieved from Huffington Post :
    http://www.huffingtonpost.com/joanne-herman/can-transgender-people-be_b_839703.html

Herrmann, N. (1997). What is the functioon of the various brainwaves. *Scientific American* .

Hickey, P. (2011, October 8). *Homosexuality: The Mental Illness that Went Away* . Retrieved from
    Behaviorism and Mental Health :
    http://www.behaviorismandmentalhealth.com/2011/10/08/homosexuality-the-mental-illness-
    that-went-away/

Meisner, G. (2012, May 22). *Golden Ratio point of the Earth*. Retrieved from Phi=1.68 The Golden
    Number : http://www.goldennumber.net/golden-ratio-of-earth/

Newberg, A. (n.d.). *How does meditation and prayer change the brain?* . Retrieved from Andrew
    Newberg Professor and Director of research Myrna Brind Center of Intergrative Medicine
    Thomas Jefferson University and Hospital : http://www.andrewnewberg.com/research/

The Authors. Journal of Child Pyschology and Psychiatry . (2015). *Borderline personality disorder*. John
    Wiley & Sons Ltd .

Weiss, H. W. (2003). The golden mean as clock cycle of brain waves . *Science Direct* , 11.

William McConochie, P. (2010, July 10). *Decline in Average IQ*. Retrieved from Global IQ 1950-2050:
    http://uhaweb.hartford.edu/BRBAKER/

World Health Organization. (1980). ICD-!0. In *International Classification of Mental & Behavior Disorders*
    (p. 267). Herndon Virgiinia : Stylus Publishing, LLC .

www.ingramcontent.com/pod-product-compliance
Lightning Source LLC
Chambersburg PA
CBHW040310010626
45792CB00022B/35